Biggles and I

Bradley Dunbar

Mudskipper Press, 2023

Paperback edition

ISBN 978 1 912226 34 4

Contents

Contents

Contents

Biggles is Bad?

I first realised that there might be something wrong with Biggles when I was aged about seventeen. Up until that point, I had always considered him a fine, upstanding example of British manhood: gallant; resourceful; brave. Someone who exhibited all those characteristics that have exemplified the very essence of what it has historically meant to be British: honourable; stoic; modest. But, all of a sudden, my eyes were opened to a new possibility. All of a sudden, Biggles might be bad.

At the time, I was working as a Saturday lad in my local bookshop. I was studying for my 'A' Levels at school, and the work in the bookshop—as well as being thoroughly enjoyable—was a useful credit on my CV prior to applying to university, as well as a means of supplementing my modest pocket money.

On the pavement, outside the bookshop, and fair weather permitting, there would be set up a trestle table upon which were laid several open-top cardboard boxes filled with cheap second-hand paperbacks. A rummage box, stocked with nothing of such value that it would be missed if it got pinched, but enticing enough that it might encourage a few would-be passers-by to stop in their tracks and be encouraged to look in and maybe buy something else. As a Saturday lad, my tasks were varied—or so I thought at the time. Now, with the benefit of hindsight, I can see that they were strictly limited to such jobs as those where I could cause the minimum amount of damage—packing; processing library books; and, occasionally, operating the cash till.

The fateful day when I discovered that Biggles might be bad, I was standing behind the front counter of the bookshop, in sole charge of the till. It was a grave responsibility; one that was weighing heavy on my youthful shoulders. I was keen to make a good impression; hopeful of a big sale that would prove my worth. A middle-aged woman came through the door, three paperback books in her hand. Three books from the rummage box, at twenty-five pence each.

"Found a bargain?" I asked.

My attempt at conversation was met with a cool, icy glare. I noticed the three books she was holding were all Biggles paperbacks, published by Armada. I had three similar books on my bookshelf back home. Here, surely, was a point of connection? I tried again:

"Fan of Biggles are you?"

The innocent comment provoked an extraordinary transformation in the middle-aged woman. Her face turned bright red, and she was momentarily rendered speechless, before managing to splutter in a voice pitched high by incandescent fury:

"A fan of Biggles! A fan of Biggles! I am only buying these books in order to burn them."

And, with that, she slapped down a handful of coins on the counter top, and marched directly out of the shop without waiting for her change, her sacrificial offerings clutched firmly in her hand.

It seemed an extraordinary reaction. We were into *Fahrenheit 451* territory. What was it in the harmless adventure stories that I had read as a child, which could possibly have given rise to such a display of passionate and confrontational emotions? At first, I was prepared to dismiss the angry fire-starter as just another example of the kind of eccentric customer, which bookshops have a habit of attracting. But, later that evening, I was still thinking about the incident, and I began to wonder if there might not be something more to it. I started asking questions—questions to friends; questions to family—and I was surprised at some of the answers that I got back.

"Biggles? Isn't he a bit racist?"

Biggles? Racist? I had never given the idea a thought.

"Biggles? Isn't he a misogynist?"

Biggles? A misogynist? I had had to look that up to find out what it meant—remember, I was only seventeen at the time, and English Language was not one of the 'A' Levels I was studying.

"Biggles? Isn't that all a bit colonialist?"

Biggles? A colonialist? Well, was that such a bad thing? I still had a lot to learn.

I began to wonder if the angry woman customer had been viewing Biggles in these same disreputable terms, too. Was it possible that my childhood hero had feet of clay?

If any were needed, it seemed like a good excuse to re-read the books in order to find out.

Biggles Who?

Has anyone not heard of Biggles? Well, increasingly, the answer to that question must surely be 'yes'. Biggles made his first appearance in 1932, and was a household name throughout most of the successive decades up until the 1980s. But, today? Biggles popularity tends to live on only in the care of a handful of middle-aged men, whose lives he influenced when they were children.

James Bigglesworth, popularly known as 'Biggles', is the creation of author Captain W. E. Johns. He has appeared in over one hundred novels and collections of short stories. A pilot by profession, his career can be split up into four distinct periods: flying as a fighter-pilot in the Royal Flying Corps during the First World War; exploring the world as a gentleman-adventurer during the inter-War years; operating as commanding officer of RAF 666 Squadron during the Second World War; and then working as a detective in the Special Air Police division of Scotland Yard, specialising in aviation-related crimes for the remainder of his career.

Born in India in 1899, he was the son of the Assistant Commissioner of the United Provinces of India. As a child, he was a rather sickly boy, prone to frequent bouts of fever and, by the time he reached his teenage years, he was sent to Britain to study at his father's alma mater, Merton Hall. At the time, Biggles seemed destined for a career, following in the footsteps of his father in the Indian Civil Service, but then war intervened.

Biggles quickly volunteered to join the recently-formed Royal Flying Corps, the air arm of the British Army, and the precursor to the Royal Air Force. Here, Biggles was emulating the career path of his creator: W. E. Johns was commissioned into the Royal Flying Corps in September 1917. Biggles proves himself to be a brave and able aviator; victor in many air combats; a natural leader of men. His most famous wartime exploits take place while a member of 266 Squadron, where he flew Sopwith Camel biplanes, leaving the service at the end of the war having been awarded the DSO and the Military Cross and bar.

After the First World War, and typical of many other young men, Biggles finds it difficult to adapt to civilian life. He continues to pursue a career in aviation, but working as a kind of freelance adventurer, accepting commissions that take him to the far corners of the earth; a fact reflected in some of the titles of the novels from that period: *Biggles Flies West*; *Biggles Flies South*; *Biggles Flies North*. Here we find Biggles engaged in activities as various as tracking down pirate gold in the Caribbean; attempting to find a mythical lost oasis in the middle of the Egyptian desert; and establishing a charter airline in the snowy wastes of Canada.

In 1939, the advent of the Second World War effectively puts an end to a potentially feckless life of misadventure, and Biggles returns to active service, taking up the post of Commanding Officer of 666 Squadron in the RAF, flying Supermarine Spitfires, where he once again acquits himself to great credit, flying missions during the Battle of Britain; and taking up arms in battlefields as diverse as Norway and Borneo.

The end of the war brings a similar dilemma to the one he had to face in 1918. However, older, and perhaps wiser, Biggles opts to continue to serve his country by helping to establish a special division of Scotland Yard, where he acts as a 'flying detective', investigating crimes in which aviation places a particular role. As well as maintaining the security of the borders of his own country, he quickly discovers the increasing internationalism of crime, and his new role leads to an even greater exploration of the globe, as is once again reflected in the book titles: *Biggles in Australia*; *Biggles in the Gobi*; *Biggles in Mexico*.

Ironically, an unfinished novel, *Biggles Does Some Homework*, finally sees Biggles preparing to retire, but his creator, W. E. Johns, died before completing the book, although the twelve completed chapters were published in 1997.

I am conscious that this is very much a 'bare-bones' biography. For anyone interested in a fictionalised account of Biggles' life and career, there is John Pearson's *Biggles: The Authorised Biography* (Sidgwick and Jackson, 1978). Similarly, for those interested in the life of his creator, Peter Beresford Ellis and Piers Williams have written *By Jove, Biggles! The Life of Captain W. E. Johns* (W. H. Allen, 1981). However, I am not attempting to elucidate every life-event in the career of James Bigglesworth. As my own book title makes clear, Biggles is required to share this book with someone else. And that second person's ego is no less important to this story than his own.

Reading #1: *Biggles Hits the Trail*

Biggles Hits the Trail was the first Biggles book that I ever read. And what an introduction to the series. Nowadays, I am fortunate enough to own a second edition hardback of this title published by Oxford University Press in 1935, but the actual book that I first read as a child was an Armada paperback, published in 1969, and priced at 3'6. The front cover of that old paperback has a dramatic picture of Biggles drop-kicking a Chung on top of a rocky ledge, against a backdrop of high, snow-covered Himalayan mountains. Almost everything that anyone could wish to know about Biggles in encapsulated in that single image. He is wearing his flying helmet and fur-lined flying jacket—sign of the aviator; he is single-handedly vanquishing a foreign foe; and he is in a land far-flung from England's Green and Pleasant.

As Hilary Mantel wrote in *The Guardian* on 12 December 2009 "…every Biggles book is a history and geography lesson." and in *Biggles Hits the Trail* we certainly get the geography lesson. Never again would I have to consider the meaning of terms such as 'scree' or 'shale' until being taken on a geography field-trip at my Grammar School, and certainly 'terminal moraine' was not a topic on my radar until well into my 'O' Levels, but here they all are in *Biggles Hits the Trail*: "Moraine. This was a glacier not many years ago, I'll warrant." (p. 87). And, if that is not enough, just for good measure, something of a chemistry lesson is included, too. The rationale for Biggles to suddenly shoot off on an expedition to

Tibet is to discover a mountain, which is reputed to be a rich source of radium, an element possessed of unusual properties, and of both scientific and monetary value: "There must be a tremendous amount of radium—if it is radium—in that mountain to produce such an effect. At today's value the man who owned it could buy the rest of the world." (p. 80). It is a topic, which W. E. Johns returns to in *Biggles and the Deep Blue Sea* (Brockhampton Press, 1968).

However, I don't want to give the impression that *Biggles Hits the Trail* is nothing more than a turgid classroom textbook. Far from it. Readers encounter a thrilling adventure story, including mysterious blue death rays; enemies who can make themselves invisible; giant, flesh-eating centipedes—and this, four decades before the similarly terrifying razor-teethed condom-maggots in *Doctor Who and the Green Death*; and, of course, a fiendish plot to take over the world.

Not that I knew it at the time of first reading, but *Biggles Hits the Trail* is actually rather atypical for a Biggles book, reading, as it does, as much like a science fiction story as a traditional adventure yarn. Johns, of course, was no stranger to science fiction later in his writing career, penning a series of novels featuring Rex Clinton in various escapades around the universe, with titles like *To Worlds Unknown* and *The Death Rays of Ardilla* and *The Edge of Beyond*. The outlandish elements of *Biggles Hits the Trail* may have much to do with the setting of the book. In 1935, the Himalayas and the Tibetan plateau would have still been places sufficiently remote to the average man, that almost anything could be imagined possible there. The Western popularisation of the region did not truly happen until the 1950s with Edmund Hillary and Tenzing Norgay's first ascent of Mount Everest in 1953; Heinrich Harrer's publication of *Seven Years in Tibet* in 1952; and the *Daily Mail's* Snowman Expedition to search for the Yeti in 1954. Amidst the backdrop of the story that Johns creates, invisibility and death rays seem perfectly plausible; no mean achievement when the author is at pains to describe his location in as much authentic detail as possible: "Once they passed a slowly moving line of men, driving heavy, bovine yaks, the animals that are used as beasts of burden on the great plateau." (p. 64). As an adult rereading the book, this is what most strikes me: Johns makes no attempt to dumb down his descriptions for a junior audience. As a child reading the same book, this was what I most enjoyed about the Biggles books: there was no suspicion that the author was patronising his reader. So, we find a 'good' character who is also a recovering opium addict; we have sage advice about looking after the planet: "Treat Nature with respect and she will tolerate you, even encourage you; but treat her with contempt, and your days are numbered." (p. 10); and we discover a typically detailed description of technical aeronautical specifications: "It was, to all intents and purposes, a flying boat, but fitted with a wheel-landing chassis which could be raised or lowered at the will of the pilot. The two 'Hercules' air-cooled engines were mounted between the planes, one on either side of the hull, in accordance with orthodox design and practice." (p. 55).

And Biggles? What do we learn about him? Well, he can be quite caustic and sarcastic, and he is prone to being rather short-tempered, and not someone who suffers fools gladly: "…after the events of the last few days his temper was inclined to be a trifle short." (p. 231). But, he can also be contemplative: "The scene was so indescribably beautiful that even Biggles held his breath." (p. 160). And he embodies all the characteristics, which he in turn believes typify the early pioneers of flight: "…courage, modesty and faithfulness." (p. 10). But what about those other matters? The racism? The charges of colonialism? The Chungs—an imaginary race of apparent East Asian descent—make an easy target for several ripe Biggles' colloquialisms: "…yellow-faced dacoit." (p. 172) and "…benighted heathens." (p. 182) being not the most offensive of them. Reading the book as a child, I passed over these racial slurs without a second thought and, even as an adult, I find myself making allowances for them, putting them in the context of their time, and weighing them against all the positive influences of the book, but I am conscious that I may not be best placed to critically assess their contemporary significance. As the Jesuits wisely say: "Give me a child till he is seven years old, and I will show you the man." My seven-year old self was already steeped in Biggles lore; it would be foolish to expect my adult self not to be in some way prejudiced by these influences from my formative years. For the sake of balance, I recognise that a second voice might be required; a reviewer who will not be afraid to speak out against my most blatant bias. With this in mind, I have decided to pick out of my past the angry woman book-burner from my bookshop days, and bring her along for the ride. She will provide my conscience; be the devil/angel on my shoulder. And, given her growing importance within this book, it seems only right that I should give her a name—albeit a fictional one—rather than keep on referring to her as the angry woman book-burner. I have decided on Mildred—a *Fahrenheit 451* reference, although a decidedly mean-spirited one. A more generous individual might have christened her Clarisse, but the woman that I remember from that so-brief encounter across a bookshop counter was definitely more a Mildred than ever she was a Clarisse, so Mildred it shall be. And, if I am being equal-handed in my criticism of *Biggles Hits the Trail*, I would have to admit that Mildred might have another contender to add to her bonfire.

I find the end of *Biggles Hits the Trail* quite interesting from a moral viewpoint. Biggles is preparing to commit genocide on an industrial scale—admittedly in the best interests of the 'civilised' world, but genocide, nevertheless. But, then, just before Biggles is required to be the person who makes the conscious decision to 'press the button', Nature, in the raw, intervenes, and takes the decision out of his hands: "Biggles took one look and saw that he was right; the lightning had fired the fuse." (p. 233). Johns making some far-seeing comment about the future climate emergency, or Johns ducking away from making Biggles appear a mass-murderer? Good God, there is an entire book's worth of veritable discussion just there.

And how did this glimpse of casual genocide affect me as a child? I think that I can truthfully reply, not in the slightest. However, I am quite prepared to concede that Mildred may disagree with me.

My Childhood Bookshelf

From a very young age, I had always been an avid reader, and this despite—or maybe because of—being brought up in a brief educational age that worshipped at the altar of Phonics. I was fortunate enough to be sufficiently critically-minded that I questioned the correct spelling of words even then––precocious brat that I was—but some of my less-seditious contemporaries have never recovered from their childhood 'say what you see' education, such that they have remained practically analphabetic throughout their entire adult lives.

There was a long list of authors and stories, which I would eagerly devour, frequently reading an entire novel at one sitting. Although this may sound like the behaviour of a priggish child, or someone with more fictional friends than actual ones, I should perhaps confess that my reading matter at the time was rarely what might be called 'educational' or 'instructional' or even 'self-improving'. I tended to shun the established classics of the children's canon of literature, like *The Swiss Family Robinson* by Johann David Wyss or C. S. Lewis' *The Chronicles of Narnia* or the stories of Peter Pan by J. M. Barrie or Charles Kingsley's *The Water-Babies;* rarely read any of the specially abridged versions of adult-approved favourites, such as Dickens' *David Copperfield*, or Stevenson's *Treasure Island* or Defoe's *Robinson Crusoe*; nor did I find myself particularly inspired by some of the more contemporary books, which were recommended reading at school, such as Clive King's *Stig of the Dump*, or *The Weirdstone of Brisingamen* by Alan Garner, or even Ursula Le Guin's *Earthsea* trilogy. Instead, I found myself drawn towards tales of adventure and exploration and mystery, and even more so when these stories formed part of a series of books.

So, I loved the Willard Price novels featuring Hal and Roger Hunt as teenager adventurers, who travelled the globe encountering wild animals, and which had titles like *Amazon Adventure* and *Volcano Adventure* and *Tiger Adventure*. I collected the Hardy Boys series of mysteries by Franklin W. Dixon, and would avidly await the release of a new paperback copy, thrilling at their titles: *The Haunted Fort*; *The Mystery at Devil's Paw*; *The Clue of the Screeching Owl*. I remember anticipating with particular relish one book called *While the Clock Ticked*, which I thought sounded enigmatically spooky and then, of course, found myself inevitably slightly disappointed when I eventually read the ensuing story. And I read the Three Investigators novels, which were marketed as though they were written by Alfred Hitchcock but were actually written by Robert Arthur, Jr., and featured junior detectives Jupiter Jones, Peter Crenshaw and Bob Andrews, and which, like the Hardy Boys, had suitably evocative titles to seduce a susceptible young reader: *The Mystery of the Screaming Clock*; *The Mystery of the Singing Serpent*; *The Mystery of the Stuttering Parrot.* Just thinking about them now makes me want to go back and reread some of them again.

So, it would seem entirely natural for Biggles, who combined all the adventure of the Hardy Boys stories, the intrigue of the Three Investigators, and the far-flung destinations of the Willard Price books, to find his own place on my childhood bookshelf alongside my other favourites.

And yet it still required an initial introduction. Someone to wave that first Biggles book under my nose and to recommend it to me. And the person who gave me that first introduction to the Biggles stories was my dad.

My dad was born in 1929. His birth certificate states that he was born in Harrow in the district of Hendon. The same document manages to misspell his name, though, so it throws a slight element of doubt over the veracity of the entire record. He was born the elder—by a matter of minutes—of twin, non-identical boys into a fairly traditional, working-class family, living in north London.

My dad was born with a slight deformity of his leg, which required him to wear splints for his earliest years; a treatment, which obviously had the required corrective effect, since he became captain of his school football and cricket teams when he was older. It was a deformity, though, which changed the course of his life. His birth parents were unable to afford the cost of bringing up two children, particularly one that required regular medical treatment, and so the two twins were separated at a very early age: my dad was brought up by his uncle and aunt; while his twin brother remained with his true parents. The two families lived close together, so the separation was not as dramatic as it might have proved, and the twins went to the same schools and saw each other regularly; nevertheless, slight variations in upbringing and outlook were inevitable.

Both families were poor. Not the grinding poverty of many families living in London at that time, but the 'watch-the-pennies' hardship of many more. My dad's 'real' dad worked as a gardener; his adopted dad as a photographer. Both twins worked hard at school. My dad was inclined towards mathematics and the sciences; his brother, my uncle, was more artistic and gifted musically. My dad was not a particularly fast or enthusiastic reader. However, he made two exceptions. The William books of Richmal Crompton, and the Biggles books of Captain W. E. Johns. But, there was a problem. The Biggles books were expensive. Published in thick—and I mean house-brick thick—hardback volumes, first by John Hamilton and then by Oxford University Press, the cover price of new volumes were typically three shillings and sixpence; sometimes four shillings. At the time, it was a sum beyond the ken of my dad's imagination. And so, the only occasion when my dad ever received a new Biggles book was at Christmas time and it would be a present beyond all expectations; as my dad later described: "The best of Christmas presents." Even then, the arrival of a new Biggles book could not be guaranteed. It depended on such variable quantities as whether my grandad had had 'a good year', or if a distant, but more wealthy, relative was sufficiently enlightened to realise the preferred reading matter of the average growing boy. I can identify with this same predicament entirely: on how many occasions as a child did I open a heavy, gift-wrapped parcel from an elderly aunt with naïve optimism, only to encounter nothing more thrilling than a depressingly worthy volume of illustrated Bible stories.

Reading #2: *The Rescue Flight*

First published just prior to the start of the Second World War, the events recounted in *The Rescue Flight* actually take Biggles back some twenty years, and to the period when he was still engaged in aerial combat over the war-ravaged battlefields of France, during the First World War. Whereas many of the books that recount Biggles' exploits as a fighter pilot during this period take the form of short stories—such as *The Camels are Coming* (John Hamilton, 1932) and *Biggles of the Camel Squadron* (John Hamilton, 1934)—*The Rescue Flight* is unusual for being a full-length novel, which is a format that I generally prefer.

The story is the tale of two brothers, Nigel and Peter Fortymore, known as Forty and Thirty. When Nigel is reported missing in action, the resourceful Peter immediately leaves the school where he has been a pupil, manages to hoodwink a passage to France for himself, and enrols in a fighter squadron, with the express intention of tracking down where Nigel is being held as a prisoner of war in Germany and bringing him home. It might sound like a forlorn hope, but Peter is fortunate enough that the squadron that he finds himself attached to is commanded by none other than James Bigglesworth, and he soon has some experienced hands to help him with his plan.

Although Biggles plays a key role in *The Rescue Flight*, it is very much Peter's story, and many of the escapades of daring-doing, which would normally fall to Biggles, are here undertaken by Peter. It is a breathless story, involving a number of landings 'behind the lines' in enemy-occupied territory, not to mention several aerial dog-fights, which Johns describes with the authenticity of detail of one who has 'been there, done that'. Typical of many Biggles books, Johns includes footnotes when he wants to explain a specialised term or some technical detail, rather than hold up the flow of the story by introducing a lengthy fact-dump. So, here, we get elucidations of such words as the 'Scarf ring': "…the gun-mounting which completely encircled the gunner's cockpit." (p. 133), plus an explanation of the 'colour of the night' and the 'letter of the night' signalling codes used by both sides as a means of identifying friend from foe during night sorties; and a slightly more whimsical muse about the glow from an airplane's exhaust pipe.

One adversary that both Peter and Biggles find themselves pitted against is the leader of the famous *Staffel*, known as the Richthofen Circus, flying Albatros DVs, out of an airbase close to Douai. The real-life Richthofen Circus was commanded by the German air ace Baron Manfred von Richthofen, popularly known as The Red Baron, because of the distinctive, brightly coloured plane that he flew.

Von Richthofen was respected as one of the greatest ever fighter pilots, officially credited with 80 combat victories. He was eventually shot down and killed on 21 April 1918, his plane crashing close to the village of Vaux-sur-Somme. Amongst many decorations, one award that von Richthofen won was the *Pour Le Mérite*, one of Prussia's highest awards, unofficially known as the Blue Max after pilot Max Immelmann, who was the first recipient of the honour during the First World War. As a boy, *The Blue Max* was one of my favourite movies. Produced in 1966, it was an unusual movie for the times, depicting the First World War from a German perspective and taking as its lead character a German air ace who is determined to rack up as many air combat victories as he is able, in order to secure for himself the coveted Blue Max. The lead role of Leutnant Bruno Stachel is taken by American actor George Peppard, who portrays the airman as a ruthless, self-obsessed individual, more concerned with self-aggrandisement than declining notions of honour and chivalry. It is interesting in *The Rescue Flight*, that a captured German spy who gives Biggles his parole and then backtracks on his word, ultimately meets with a sticky end: "From far away, so far that they could only just hear it, came the mutter of a machine-gun. The drone of the engine died away. Silence fell." (p. 249). Johns has noted that the concept of 'honour' in warfare is becoming outdated, however it is obviously a belief that he still considers important, so while Biggles and his compatriots still fight by the airborne equivalent of the Queensberry Rules, it is only ever their enemies who are prepared to sink sufficiently to deliver a 'low blow'.

For a book that has as its central character a teenage protagonist, *The Rescue Flight* deals with a number of complex adult themes in a surprisingly nuanced way: life and death; loyalty and honour; both the glory and the futility of war. Johns does not shirk away from descriptions of violent death: "...his legs seemed to fold up under him and he crashed to the ground like a wet overcoat falling from a peg." (p. 94), nor does he patronise his juvenile audience, although he is sometimes guilty of replacing feelings of fear with feelings of fascination: "Thirty could only watch, like a bird fascinated by a snake. 'He's shooting at me,' he thought—but still he did nothing." (p. 38); and "His heart seemed to stop beating, as with a sort of spellbound fascination, he waited for what appeared to be a wholesale collision." (p. 105). Another emotion, and one which is frequently returned to in other Biggles books, is that of loneliness: "The Bristol was alone in a lonely world of its own." (p. 90). Alan Sillitoe entitled a famous short story *The Loneliness of the Long-Distanced Runner*, but *The Loneliness of the Long-Distance Aviator* would be equally appropriate. Biggles, later in life, flying in peacetime, often comments on the sense of isolation, being a tiny speck amidst a vast emptiness of sky. In wartime, Johns very effectively contrasts these same moments of introspection and solitude with ones of frantic, breathless action, and a sky, which far from being empty is instead: "…full of machines." (p. 240) and where there was simply not the time to think between instinct and action.

Peter 'Thirty' Fortymore enters the war full of youthful idealism; by the end of the book, his attitude has changed. He realises that he does not even know what it is that everyone is fighting over: "For the first time he began to perceive what war really meant; he felt the relentlessness of it—the ruthlessness, the waste, the cruelty, the incredible folly of it." (p. 224). I think that if Mildred was sufficiently dispassionate, she might even be prepared to mark this one up as a plus point to the credit of W. E. Johns. A book for keeping, rather than one for burning. Johns has sometimes been criticised for his glorification of war, but this could not be further from the truth. Johns was vocally and vociferously anti-war, as only someone who has experienced active conflict can be, and he actively advocated peace through a mutual understanding of nations and a "toleration of each others' national characteristics." (*Popular Flying*, May 1933)

Ultimately, though, *The Rescue Flight* retains as its central premise the bond between brothers: "Hitherto he had regarded the war as something impersonal; something which was best regarded in the abstract. Now the war meant him and Forty." (p. 225). And, as Thirty passionately declares: "'I'd do anything to save my brother—*anything*.'" (p. 216). It would be easy at this point to make a neat segue between the relationship that existed between the brothers Thirty and Forty in *The Rescue Flight* and that between my dad and his twin. Both suffered the same sense of separation: Thirty and Forty's occasioned by war; my dad and his twin by simple economics. However, it would be to display a sentimentality unworthy of W. E. Johns to attempt to extend the analogy any further. The simple fact was that the circumstances that each set of brothers found themselves in was different. Wartime and fiction produce heroes, who are vaunted and glamorised and showered in medals; peacetime and reality produce heroes who are understated and undecorated and who pass relatively unnoticed, and my dad was all the more a hero for that.

A Few Friends in Need of an Introduction

Biggles was rarely a 'lone ranger' in any of his books—*Biggles Goes Alone* a notable exception—and was invariably accompanied in his adventures by a band of loyal friends, most notably Algy, Ginger and, later, Bertie, and it would seem only right that they receive some kind of introduction of their own.

The Honourable Algernon Montgomery Lacey is a distant cousin of Biggles, and he is first encountered in the short story called 'The Boob', which was published in the September 1932 edition of *Popular Flying Magazine*, and later formed one of the stories in the first Biggles book, *The Camels are Coming.* Biggles first impression of Algy is not very favourable, but when Algy acquits himself with great bravery flying in a combat mission, Biggles opinion quickly changes and the two men become firm friends and inseparable comrades in arms. Algy's role in the Biggles books tends to be as Biggles' dependable second-in-command; as such, he is often left in the less-than-glamorous position of 'holding the fort' whilst Biggles goes off engaged in more exciting adventures. But every hero needs their sidekick, and so Algy is 'Robin' to Biggles' 'Batman'; 'Goose' to Biggles' 'Maverick'; 'Gromit' to Biggles' 'Wallace'.

Ginger Hebblethwaite is a young protégé of Biggles, who first appeared in the novel *The Black Peril* (Hamilton, 1935). His real first name is never revealed in the books, and he is known simply as 'Ginger' because of his shock of red-coloured hair. A teenage runaway, Ginger is taken under Biggles' care, and is given instruction of how to be a pilot; the opening chapter of *Biggles Hits the Trail* sees Biggles, Algy and Ginger celebrating the occasion of Ginger being awarded his Royal Aero Club Pilot's 'A' Licence. Ginger often infuriates Biggles by talking in Americanisms that he has learned from the cinema, but he is invariably Biggles companion-of-choice when action is required.

The third of Biggles principal comrades is Lord Bertie Augustus Lissie, who first appears in the short story 'So This is War', which featured in the February 1940 issue of *Air Stories* magazine. Bertie's first appearance in book-form is in *Spitfire Parade* (Oxford University Press, 1941). Bertie is an aristocrat and former racing driver, wears a perpetual monocle, and is possessed of more courage than common sense, but he is a loyal follower and friend of Biggles, and occupies the position of the comic foil in most of the later Biggles novels.

Most of the books in the Biggles chronology, which come after *Spitfire Parade* tend to feature all three of Biggles' companions to a greater or lesser degree; the four men all share rooms in Mount Street in Mayfair; and all four find employment with Scotland Yard after the Second World War.

The friendship between the four men is an important part of the books, although it is typically unsentimental and undemonstrative. British stiff-upper-lip does not permit any great expressions of affection. So, we might see Ginger showing his admiration for Biggles, or Biggles teasing Bertie about some faux-pas he has made, but there is rarely any great outpouring of public emotions even when, as sometimes happened, one or other of the quartet was reported missing, feared dead. A rare display of raw emotions appears in *The Rescue Flight*, when the headmaster of the school that the brothers Nigel and Peter Fortymore attend as pupils learns that Nigel has been reported presumed dead in First World War France: "The Head's face was buried in his hands. His shoulders were shaking. Thirty stared. A sense of unreality swept over him. The whole thing was a dream. It was preposterous—the Head, of all people, blubbing." (*The Rescue Flight*, p. 12). The episode is clearly drawn from a real-life experience, when Johns visited his old headmaster, Major G. W. Kinman at his old school, Hertford Grammar School, at the end of the First World War.

However, more often than not, the limit of emotion that Johns permits to enter his narrative is a modest gesture, as when Algy and Biggles part during a conflict in the Middle East: "Their hands met in a firm grip, the only time during the whole war that either of them had allowed their real feelings to get uppermost." (*Biggles Flies East*, p. 152). So, while there might be many valuable life-lessons, which can be gleaned from the Biggles books, they are never going to find their way onto the 'relationship self-help' sections of any bookshops, nor will Biggles himself win any awards as an agony aunt or for best listening ear. The friendships in the Biggles books tend to be ones that have been forged by tackling and overcoming a shared adversity, and based on loyalty, courage and as young Peter Fortymore is apt to quote in *The Rescue Flight*: "Through thick and thin."

And One Enemy, Too

It is impossible to have the kind of life and career that Biggles had without breaking a few eggs along the way. And, in Biggles case, most of those eggs seem to have got broken on top of the head of one man: Erich von Stalhein.

Biggles first encounters von Stalhein in *Biggles Flies East* (Oxford University Press, 1935), where the Prussian is a Hauptmann, working for the German Intelligence Staff in the Middle East during the First World War. Von Stalhein presents a tall, upright figure, with "…cold brooding eyes that were hard to meet and held a steel-like quality that the monocle he habitually wore could not dispel." (*Biggles Flies East*, p. 36). One other distinctive physical characteristic is that "…he walked with a permanent limp with the aid of two sticks, and this physical defect added something to his sinister bearing." (*Biggles Flies East*, p. 36). However, von Stalhein is not someone to be underestimated, as Biggles knows only too well. He is clever, resourceful and utterly ruthless; a worthy adversary, whom Biggles encounters regularly throughout his career; the two men pitted against each other during both World Wars, and then later during the Cold War, when von Stalhein finds employment working on the Russian side of the Iron Curtain.

Even the greatest enmity must eventually come to an end, though, and the one between Biggles and von Stalhein does so in surprising fashion. Pre-empting the end of the Cold War by some thirty years—although not foreseeing the recent rise in tensions again occasioned by Russia's invasion of Ukraine—in *Biggles Buries a Hatchet* (Brockhampton, 1958), Biggles is tasked with rescuing his old adversary from a Sakhalin concentration camp, after which a grateful von Stalhein settles in England, finding work as a translator, and embarks on a slightly strained, but nevertheless respectful friendship with the man who had for so long been a constant thorn in his side.

Reading #3: *Biggles Flies East*

If anyone were to conduct a straw-poll of the most popular Biggles book, I would be prepared to bet that *Biggles Flies East* would appear somewhere near the top, if not at the very summit.

Set during the First World War, the scene of conflict transfers from the relentless struggle fought above and amidst the trenches of Europe, to the espionage and intrigues occurring in the Middle East, with Biggles co-opted from his fighter squadron in France to take up duties as a double agent in Palestine, taking the identity of disgraced defector Lieutenant Leopold Brunow. The actual place names that Johns uses in the book are fictional, but the setting is authentically described, as are the feelings of tension that Biggles experiences thrust into an arena of conflict, which is unfamiliar to him, in a region that is unhealthily riddled by the "...canker of espionage." (p. 108).

Biggles Flies East is not without humour, though; in fact, I find it one of the most amusing of the entire Biggles series, particularly regarding the cat and mouse battle that plays out between Biggles and his chief adversary, Hauptmann Erich von Stalhein of the German Intelligence staff. Time and time again, von Stalhein believes that he has managed to obtain evidence in order to unmask Biggles as a double agent, only for the quick-thinking Biggles to counter with a plausible explanation and so thwart his rival. Living under this constant threat of exposure and death leads Biggles into an almost devil-may-care attitude, oscillating between states of steely calm and, at other times, near hysteria: "He was tired out, physically and mentally, yet he could not repress a smile as he thought of his own position." (p. 102). The dichotomy of his duel existence leads to moments of great irony, too: "The idea of an Englishman and a German each trying to save the other's life struck him as funny." (p. 115); and, later, when he is commanded to undertake a flying mission for the Germans: "…the idea of bombing a British aerodrome amused him." (p. 157). However, W. E. Johns does not play the entire book for laughs. Indeed, the themes of personal loneliness and the pointlessness of war, which run through many of the Biggles novels are particularly resonant here, characterised by the isolation of Biggles' position as a lone spy operating behind enemy lines, and also in the nature of the stark, empty, desert landscape, which surrounds him. The typical character of Biggles is of someone who is clubbable by nature: he enjoys the camaraderie of his fellow pilots; the support of close friends, loyal to him; working as a secret agent on his own goes against his nature: "The queer feeling of loneliness came back with renewed force, and in his heart he knew that he loathed the work he was doing more than ever." (pp. 75-76). Biggles' feelings of loneliness whilst surrounded by enemies on all sides, is very different to the sensation of isolation he feels when he is forced to crash land in the middle of the desert, alone, miles from the nearest salvation: "Once he straightened his back and looked round the scene, but its overwhelming solitude made him shudder and he went on with his task, doing his best to fight off the dreadful feeling of depression that was creeping over him." (p. 117). Here, his battle is with the natural world; to survive in an inhospitable wasteland, which is an enemy to all men alike, regardless of their allegiance to a particular country or ideology.

Johns does not wave the flag of his own patriotism with such a fervour that he is blinded to his own side's failings. In *Biggles Flies East* he acknowledges that the Germans are winning the war of espionage in the Middle East—possibly a bit of a back-handed compliment, since it is clear that he does not regard espionage as one of the higher arts—and as in *The Rescue Flight*, he is quick to show Biggles' displeasure at what he considers an act of deceit by his own superior officer: "Biggles flushed. Then his face paled. 'Then if you'll permit me to express an opinion, sir, I don't think that's good enough,' he said angrily." (*The Rescue Flight*, p. 142). It is quite an adult concept for what is ostensibly meant to be a children's book: the idea that the side you are working for might just happen to be wrong. Which brings me neatly to Mildred.

I had read practically to the end of *Biggles Flies East* and thought that there could be little here that Mildred could possibly find objection to—a couple of mildly disparaging remarks about both Arabs and Germans, but nothing that couldn't be dismissed as rough-house bants—when… The N-word. And even an alliterative use of the N-word (p. 189). I can feel the heat from the pyre grow another book hotter even from here.

One of W. E. Johns' claims to fame—not that he would have claimed it for himself—is that he rejected T. E. Lawrence when he applied to be an RAF recruit, at the time that Johns was working as a recruiting officer. Perhaps he took against someone else who conspicuously went under two initials before their name? J. K. Rowling, don't even think about applying. Actually, Lawrence applied for the position under the assumed name of John Hume Ross and Johns, seeing through the obvious deception, turned him down on the basis of submitting a false name; a decision that he was later ordered to revoke, when strings were pulled above him. I am sure that the incident must have rankled with Johns, though. In *Biggles Flies East*, a Lawrence-like figure appears fleetingly in the enigmatic 'guise of the British intelligence officer Major Sterne: "The next moment he was watching with a kind of fascinated interest a man who swept into the room, for he knew he was looking at one of the most talked-of men in the Middle East, a man whose knowledge of native law was proverbial and who could disguise himself to deceive even the Arabs themselves." (p. 241). Significantly, Sterne is unmasked as a German agent in disguise—perhaps a little jab of revenge served cold?

Oh, and it was "Nimble" (p. 189), since you're wondering.

The Seventeen and a Half Pence Paperback

At the time that I first started reading Biggles books, decimalisation had been only recently introduced. Many of the second-hand paperback copies that I picked up still had prices marked in shillings on their covers. New paperbacks were issued under either the Armada or Knight imprints, owned by publishers William Collins and Hodder and Stoughton respectively. I would routinely scour the shelves of my local branch of W. H. Smith to see if any new titles had been added to their stocks, or simply to salivate over the ones that I had yet to save up enough pocket money to afford. The typical price of a new paperback was seventeen and a half pence. It was a considerable sum for someone whose weekly pocket money wasn't counted in double figures.

So, why didn't I simply take out the books I wanted from my local public library? Looking back, it is a question that is hard to answer. Perhaps my family were simply not habitual library-goers? Although I do recall that both my mum and I did possess library cards. I think it was more that I had a certain prejudice about the library—one that I still retain to this day. I find them rather depressing places, more like a graveyard for books rather than somewhere to celebrate the written word. I don't like the way that libraries put their own labels inside books, and their stickers on the spines; I like my volumes to be unsullied by these appendages of bureaucratic vandalism. More, I want to feel the thrill of possession; to hold in my hand a book, which I know belongs to me, and that I don't have to return by the following week. I want to own the author's work; experience a connection with it that I can't do knowing that countless anonymous date-stamps have already shared it before me. Is it at this point that I should reveal that I am an only child? Even to my ears, these sound like the kind of sentiments that I can imagine that only an only child might make; the kind of kid who has not had to think about sharing any of their possessions with either older or younger siblings. Whatever, I can't change that aspect of who I am and, by going on to eventually work in a bookshop, my mistrust of the library only tended to increase; I rarely considered that we were both in our different ways serving a wider book-reading community; it felt more as though the library was our direct rival, taking consumer coppers out of our commercial pockets by offering up their goods for free.

In contrast to the library, the bookshops of my youth were pleasure palaces for me. And the bookcases of children's novels were always so appealing with their brightly coloured spines and evocative titles. For this kid, it was his equivalent of the candy shop.

The halfpenny coin was removed from circulation in Britain by the Treasury in 1984, with Chancellor Nigel Lawson saying that: "most people would be glad to get rid of them." I, for one, was not one of those people. Those halfpennies were important to me. I used to collect them in a jar; frequently putting them in piles to count them up, in the hope that I was approaching some magical sum, like a pound—it never was. And they provided an all-important buffer to any potentially spiralling costs to my Biggles books. My economic reasoning ran along these lines: seventeen and one half pence was a very precise sum to charge for a book. It was clearly a considered figure, carefully calculated to take into account all of the associated costs of the production of the book, pay the author his royalties, any expenses for marketing and distribution, to leave a small margin left over as profit. Presumably the halfpenny. That halfpenny on every book represented the publisher's margin, and who was I to begrudge them that? Lose the halfpenny, though, and where were we? I was under no illusion that the price of my favourite books would be simply rounded up to the next penny and so come out at eighteen pence each. Oh, no. I was already sufficiently savvy to recognise how the world of business worked. It would be twenty pence at the very least; more likely the neat sum of twenty-five pence; and then, after twenty-five pence, where did it go from there? Thirty, forty, fifty, the sky was the limit. And I was proved not so very wrong in my worst-case economic predictions: when Knight published a paperback edition of *Biggles and the Little Green God* in 1979 it was priced on the back cover at sixty-five pence. Sixty-five pence! It was daylight robbery. A price pegged sufficiently high to have me considering the possibility of returning to the library. Almost, but not quite.

Biggles Rebranded

I have always been someone who is rather resistant to change. I believe I am not alone in this reaction. Typically, people fall into one of three categories. Those who accept change immediately and unquestioningly; those who are resistant to change but go along with it after a period of reflection; and those who will not budge from an established position, even if to change is ultimately to their advantage. Of these, I tend to be of the middle mind-set: resistant, but not dogmatic. I consider that this is a sensible attitude. It allows for a cooling-off period of critical reflection, which can be no bad thing when making a decision. Having said that, forty years on, and I still don't like the 'new-look' Biggles paperbacks, which both Armada and Knight brought out between the late-Seventies and the early-Eighties.

I had grown accustomed to the Knight books published between the late-Sixties and the mid-Seventies: they all had a satisfying uniformity about them. The discrete Knight logo to the bottom left of the cover and at the base of the spine; author and title listed in a consistent style on the spine, and a bold, dramatic image covering the entire front cover. It was a similar story with the Armada books during the same period. Although their 'ship' logo did have a tendency to stray to different positions on the cover, the books still all looked like a set upon my bookshelf, with their colourful spines displaying publisher, title and author information, plus a small code number at the base, which supposedly meant something to someone behind the scenes at Armada HQ. However, it was an early lesson to me to discover that all good things must come to an end.

The new Knights appeared first. They were uniformly branded with an illustration of a slightly rueful-looking Biggles, complete with goggles and flying helmet in a small bubble in the top left-hand corner of the front cover, and then the title printed at a jaunty slant, and a large, colour illustration beneath, depicting a scene from the story. All things considered, it was rather a nice design—and one that I have come to appreciate more in hindsight—but, at the time, it felt like too much of a departure from the appearance of the books that I had been gradually amassing to form my own collection. The new Knights did bring with them a host of new titles, some which I had never seen published in paperback before, like *Biggles in Mexico*. However, one of the new releases went a step too far: *Biggles and the Lost Treasure*. When I first saw the paperback, I thought that it was an entirely new Biggles book. Even though I only owned a fraction of the Biggles titles that I knew to be in existence, I was pretty near fluent on being able to recite all of the books that Johns had ever written and, with the author himself having died a year after I was born, the chances of any new works being added to this list seemed remote. Yet, here was a title that I had never heard of before. Could it be that mythical beast: a brand new Biggles? A previously unpublished manuscript from the author's back catalogue, never before exposed to the public gaze? To my disappointment, it was not to be. What was actually the case was that Knight had simply retitled an existing book, *Biggles and the Lost Sovereigns*, presumably in the belief that *Lost Treasure* would make a catchier title, or that the word 'sovereign' was no longer relevant to a late Twentieth-century audience. However, to me, it just seemed a cheek. Some anonymous individual working in a publisher's marketing department thinking that they can improve on the literary decision made by the original author of the book—and I speak from a position of some knowledge, being able to also number working in a publisher's marketing department on my curriculum vitae, alongside that of working in a bookshop.

Worse was to come when Armada launched their new-look range of paperbacks. Once again, there were several titles that I had never seen before in paperback—including *Biggles Hunts Big Game* and *Biggles – Charter Pilot*; the only previous paperback editions having been issued long before I was a reader—but the design of the new books were such a departure from any that had gone before, that I couldn't reconcile myself to buying them. A red Biggles logo on a stark, white background: somehow they entirely failed to capture the essence of what Biggles meant to me. Even the reissued volume of *Biggles Hits the Trail*, which reproduced the iconic image of Biggles drop-kicking a Chung from the 1969 paperback, still failed to covert me. If I am being fair, my lack of enthusiasm for Armada's rebranding was not all down to the new design: it was the early-Eighties; I was entering my teenage years; attempting to forge for myself a new identity by casting adrift all the influences that had previously so captivated me as a child and, in so doing, it was inevitable that Biggles would prove to be a casualty—albeit not a permanent one.

However, little did I know it, but there was an even greater shock-of-the-new waiting for me just around the corner.

The Posed Photo Covers

The timing of my teenage estrangement from Biggles could hardly have proved more opportune. In the mid-Eighties, Knight would once again attempt to rejuvenate the Biggles brand, this time by issuing a series of paperbacks with posed photographic images adorning the cover. As a child, the sight of an actor posing as Biggles in khaki shorts and long white socks on the front cover of *Biggles on Mystery Island* or that of Biggles and Ginger both wearing gaudy-coloured tank-tops on the front of *Biggles Investigates* would have had me fuming. I would have been indignant; would have felt as though my life-choices were being ridiculed. But I was spared this indignity. It is only now, as an adult, that I can look back and marvel at the designs, and actually find much amusement in them.

No child likes to think they are being laughed at, and the Knight 'posed' covers must surely have struck a wrong note with an entire generation of Biggles readers. If I had been coming to Biggles anew at that particular time, I would never have given the new Knights so much as a second, contemptuous glance. In the same way that Sylvester McCoy's tenureship of Dr Who sounded a death knell for the TV programme for the next fifteen years, so the Knight poseurs signalled a decline in the fortunes of Biggles; one from which he has never recovered. Good, God, what was wrong with the 1980s? Margaret Thatcher; yuppie bankers; and, on top of all that, the Biggles posed photo covers.

The excellent and informative website biggles.com perhaps passes the most telling judgement on the new Knight covers by simply stating beneath a picture of each one: "No cover photographer is credited." This understated comment speaks volumes. They also note that: "Some of these posed photographic covers are, it has to be said, frankly ridiculous!" And none more so than the cover for *Biggles Forms a Syndicate,* which Knight published in paperback for the first time in 1984.

The photo on the front of *Biggles Forms a Syndicate* shows Biggles and Ginger carrying a large suitcase, which has been attempted to look like a medical supply chest with the aid of a bit of brown paper and two Red Cross stickers, running past an old First World War biplane. To be fair to the designer, a Tiger Moth does get a passing mention in the story, but considering the book was first published in 1961, the biplane is an anachronism when Biggles was flying Dakotas and Proctors at the time. A large, medical box does feature, too: "Everything else is there except the medicine kit, a black box, marked with a bold red cross." (*Biggles Forms a Syndicate*, p. 51) but it is hardly the most dramatic scene from the tale.

So far, so bad, although it is not the stuff of legends. What transports the cover of *Biggles Forms a Syndicate* from the merely awful to the stupendously gruesome are the frozen looks of horror on the faces of the two actors, combined with their stilted poses, as though they have been taking part in a game of Grandmother's

Footsteps—Statues, to a modern generation—and have both been caught in the process of moving. Ginger looks a bit like an anxious Harry Styles from *One Direction*; Biggles looks more like an off-duty stock broker, his mouth locked in a rictus of white-teethed determination, and is wearing a bizarre get-up of all-in-one white boiler suit, and natty matching neck scarf. On other titles, there is a Bertie, too, complete with monocle and kiss-curl.

I would like to be able to provide a postmodern interpretation of the Knight 'posed' covers. Review them with the benefit of hindsight and be able to declare that they are so bad that they are actually good. But they are not. They are so bad that they are bad. When compared to the minimalist and understated precision of Howard Leigh's cover art, such as his design for the first edition of *Biggles Flies East,* the Knight covers are a travesty.

I have contacted Hodder and Stoughton to try to fill in a few gaps in the story of the Knight covers. I would love to know the names of the actors; where the pictures were taken; who was the uncredited photographer; but no further information has been forthcoming. Perhaps "No cover photographer is credited" remains the most appropriate epitaph for them?

Reading #4: *The Black Peril*

I can feel Mildred's hackles rising just at the sound of the title of this book, but let's not rush to any hasty conclusions. To do that would be to dismiss a book, which as an adult has become my own personal favourite in the Biggles' canon. Also, there is little to be discovered here that can give cause for Mildred to complain, although this may be partly due to the fact that Johns uses a subtle analogy to convey a sweeping generalisation about national characteristics: in this case a comparison between the British and German temperament. And how does W. E. Johns perform this ingenious literary sleight of hand? By substituting dogs for humans. To set the scene: Ginger is being menaced by a "huge black Alsatian" (p. 77), which is acting as a guard dog for an enemy gang. Armed only with a stiff-bristled broom, Ginger manages to get the better of his canine adversary, instigating the observation: "Had the dog been a bulldog there could only have been one ending to such an encounter, but the Alsatian lacks the deadly dogged ferocity of its smaller brother." (p. 77). If Johns had extended this same strategy throughout all his books it might have avoided a lot of Twenty-first century political corrections of his original words. Many an insulting comment, which might be censored if it were aimed directly at China as an entire nation, could be slung at the Pekingese or the Shih Tzu without it raising complaint; similarly, many national stereotypes, which might be castigated if they appeared to be belittling the French or the

Germans, would escape comment if they fell upon the heads of Poodles or Rottweilers instead. The Afghan Hound; The Dalmatian; The Rhodesian Ridgeback; the St Bernard; the Shiba Inu: there could have been almost no limit to the potential for Johns' inventive expression, should he have chosen to go there. But, we are entering a world of counterfactuals, which brings me to an important piece of advice that Johns *does* articulate: "'Listen, my lad,' interrupted Biggles, quietly, 'never worry your head wondering what *might* have happened—that doesn't matter two hoots. Always stick to facts; they are the only things that count.'" (p. 180). It was sound counsel given the state of Europe at that time.

Adolf Hitler having been elected Chancellor of Germany in 1933 and Joseph Stalin in charge of the Soviet Union was causing a lot of what-ifs to be asked in Britain. In the middle years of the 1930s, it was not entirely clear which allegiances could be relied upon and which were likely to be broken. In his plot for *The Black Peril* (Hamilton, 1935), Johns anticipates the Molotov-Ribbentrop Pact of non-aggression between Nazi Germany and the Soviet Union by some four years, creating a story that involves the two nations conspiring together to bomb Britain.

However, leaving serious British, German and Russian inter-war politics aside, the opening chapters of *The Black Peril* resemble something closer to a French farce when considering the three main characters involved. It is a case of opening and shutting doors as we don't see Biggles, Algy and Ginger all stand together as a united trio until: "Where his bullets went Ginger did not know, nor did he stop to find out; he dropped the weapon into his pocket and dashed off in the direction taken by Biggles and Algy." (p. 80). Up until that point, we have had Biggles and Algy together and no Ginger; Biggles and Ginger together and no Algy; and then Algy and Ginger together and no Biggles. For all that, though, *The Black Peril* is Ginger's book.

Was there a time before Ginger? It is hard to believe that the young lad does not feature in any of the Biggles stories relating to the First World War; he is such a constant presence thereafter. Biggles, Algy and Ginger: the terrible trio. However, it was not always the case: reading the review of *Biggles Flies Again* (Hamilton, 1934), on the back cover of the dust wrapper for *The Black Peril,* the "popular trio" to which it refers is "Captain James

Bigglesworth, Algernon Montgomery Lacey and Smyth." Smyth? Flight-Sergeant Smyth is Biggles' loyal mechanic throughout many adventures, during both world wars and after, and indeed features heavily in the story of *The Black Peril;* but replace Ginger? In words that I can imagine could almost have been emitted from Ginger's own mouth: it was never gonna happen. Ginger is famous for his Americanisms, picked up from a childhood watching American movies at his local cinema in Smettleworth. When Biggles first meets Ginger, he is a teenage runaway, escaping the confines of a small, Northern mining town, with the ambition of reaching the bright lights of London and hopefully training to be an RAF pilot: "...my name's Habblethwaite." It is only in subsequent books that his surname is changed to the more commonly written Hebblethwaite. Of his first name: it is never revealed; Ginger becoming his accepted appellation due to his "...mop of towsled red hair." (p. 42).

Some of Ginger's Americanisms sound slightly phoney, particularly when he refers to Biggles as "baby" (p. 92) and "big boy" (p. 222) and it is perhaps just as well that Biggles comes down hard on these linguistic aberrations before they threaten to overpower his entire character. However, one thing that is evident about Ginger from *The Black Peril*, is that he is a young man who is not short of initiative and, on more than one occasion, he is the member of the trio who comes up with a masterplan in order to save the day. As Biggles himself remarks about him: "'He's brilliant is that boy! That isn't cleverness, it's genius—genius.'" (p. 167).

The first edition of *The Black Peril* is now a very rare book indeed. It benefits from having a wonderful dust wrapper designed by Howard Leigh, who also provided illustrations for the colour frontispiece of the book, plus four plates. W. E. Johns was very fortunate to collaborate with Leigh on many volumes at this time—from *The Camels are Coming* to *Biggles Sees it Through* (Oxford, 1941)—establishing an elegant and distinctive look for the entire series. Leigh was a specialist in aviation art, and an advertisement in the rear of *The Black Peril,* promotes twenty-four sepia prints of his work, all characterised by the meticulous detail of his illustrations, and covering planes as diverse as the Sopwith Pup to the Fokker D.VII. The aircraft, which adorn the front cover of *The Black Peril* are a fictional creation of W. E. Johns, but they are still rendered with great accuracy and attention to detail according to the author's imagined specifications: "It was a metal flying boat of the high-wing monoplane type, not unlike the famous Dornier Do.X, but painted black. Fared into the leading edge of the cantilever wing were eight engines, fitted with gleaming metal propellers. The exhaust manifolds were gathered into two large exhaust pipes, one on each side of the hull, that thickened strangely towards the end." (p. 31).

Just as an aside: the modern Dornier Museum occupies a contemporary glass building in Friedrichshafen on the northern shore of Lake Constance. I can't recommend a visit highly enough.

Old Pence and Cat's Piss

At the far end of the town where I grew up, away from the High Street and all of the major shops, there was a rather dark and dingy street, which was little frequented and largely forgotten. It was the home of a traditional hardware store and a rather terrifying motorcycle repair outfit; a small music shop and a photographer's studio; a proper pet shop—before they were banned—and, behind a shadowy window, which all but obscured the exact nature of the premises that lay beyond, a second-hand bookshop.

The bookshop was run by Mr Carr, or Old Mr Carr as he was always referred to. The shop was the epitome of what a second-hand bookshop should look like. Books were stacked from floor to ceiling; on dusty narrow shelves; in wildly teetering piles; in crates on the floor; on a large, trestle table, out on the pavement. There was no order to the place: no alphabetised rows; no classification by category, or subject, or even size, or colour; no attempt at documentation of the contents; no database of titles. There was no need. Old Mr Carr knew where every single book was, and could always find it when asked. It was through the auspices of Mr Carr's bookshop that I encountered my first *hardback* Biggles book; my memory fails me as to exactly which book it was; one of the old, red-boards, Hodder reprints, I think;

perhaps *Biggles Hunts Big Game* (Hodder, 1948) or *Biggles Breaks the Silence* (Hodder, 1949). Few of the books in Mr Carr's shop came complete with dust wrappers; most were covered by a thick layer of dust; some riddled by insects. Needless to say, it was a complete paradise for a book-loving boy.

None of the books in Old Mr Carr's shop had prices marked inside them, and I suspect that he just made up the prices as he went along, based on a mixture of the book's worth and the customer's ability to pay; in my case, I was rarely charged more than a few pennies. Old pennies.

That was one of Old Mr Carr's idiosyncrasies: he never followed the rest of the country into decimalisation in 1971; forever remained in a world of pounds, shillings and pence. It did not seem to matter. Whatever small change that I had in my pocket was usually accepted, and I would invariably leave Mr Carr's shop with an old Biggles book that I had never seen before, and which I couldn't obtain new in paperback.

Another habitué of Mr Carr's premises was the shop cat, Bookie: a coolly hostile black cat, who would sometimes be found curled up asleep on top of a pile of books close to the door, but whose presence was more often only detected by the small ossified turds that she left behind, and by the overpowering smell of cat's piss, which pervaded the entire establishment.

To me, Old Mr Carr was simply a very old man, rather eccentric in his ways, who had led no other life than to run the rather chaotic second-hand bookshop at the wrong end of town. But there was much more to Mr Carr than that.

In a strange twist, which links him to W. E. Johns by one degree of separation, John Taylor Carr—as Old Mr Carr was actually christened—once served under T. E. Lawrence during the First World War. Hard to picture the gentle old bookseller as a soldier; hard to imagine that he had ever once been young.

But, though he would never have known it, I can truly say that Old Mr Carr was a genuine influence on my formative years and, in a time before the internet, his iconic emporium was a gateway to a world of knowledge and entertainment otherwise inaccessible for me.

A Disappointment in Arundel

Old Mr Carr's bookshop had opened my eyes to the possibility that a hitherto hidden treasure trove of old Biggles books existed in a world, which up until that point I had been blithely unaware. But, now that I had been made privy to the glorious possibilities of the second-hand shop, I kept my eyes open for them wherever I went. I quickly established that Carr's was the only such shop in my local area, but that did not preclude the possibility of similar establishments existing in other towns. I simply needed to expand my search area. For a boy, not yet into his teens, the opportunities to undertake this task were not great. Despite the fact that aged three years old, I had once attempted to run away from home on my push-scooter, nothing but an old comic to number amongst my possessions, an old aunt in Camberwell my intended destination—a mere twenty miles' distance as the crow flies—experience had since taught me that my current Raleigh Chopper bicycle only had a range limited to my immediate neighbourhood. I was largely dependent on the whims of my family and my dad's Ford Cortina for any excursions outside of this zone; journeys, which usually found me seated on the sticky, faux leather back seat, playing I-Spy in a desperate attempt to distract myself from being car-sick.

An unexpected daytrip to Arundel in West Sussex—ostensibly to visit the Castle—had me speculating about the possibilities for increasing the size of my Biggles collection, particularly when almost the first thing we saw after we had parked the car was a quaint old bookshop, its fine bow window displaying a colourful array of old children's books with decorate pictorial boards. As bookshops went this was a very different kettle of fish to that of Old Mr Carr's. The books were arranged in nicely-ordered shelves, classified by subject; some books were protected behind glass cabinets, like prize exhibits in a museum. There was no cat; no smell of cat's piss.

I quickly discovered the children's section. The books were arranged in alphabetical order of author, but I had little need for the extra assistance; I was beginning to develop a trained eye to be able to spot a Biggles book at twenty paces. I looked over the row of volumes with a critical eye. Several books I had already obtained from Carr's; several others I owned paperback versions. But, what was this? *Biggles in the Gobi* (Hodder, 1953). I had never seen a copy before. The book had no dust wrapper; it had a red hardcover binding, black type, and an illustration of what I took to be a yak's skull on the front boards. I had heard of the Gobi. Knew it to be a distant desert, straddling China and Mongolia, and a place where a large number of fossil discoveries were routinely made. The prospect of reading about what Biggles did there was almost too exciting. I had the book off the shelf, into my hand, and was approaching the counter to pay before anyone else could snaffle this valuable prize away from my sticky grasp. This looked like being my lucky day.

But, as I have already said: this bookshop was very different from Old Mr Carr's. The man behind the counter took the book from me, eyeing me suspiciously, as though he doubted my ability to pay. To allay his fears, I reached into my trouser pocket and withdrew its contents, proudly displaying my entire life's fortune: a burgeoning collection of two pence, one pence and halfpenny pieces; there must have been almost fifty pence there in total. Enough, surely, to buy practically half of the stock of his bookshop if I should have so chosen?

The man behind the counter, glanced inside the front page of the book. There was a small, pencilled figure written there; I hadn't even thought to check, such was my excitement.

"That will be two pounds, please."

I asked him to repeat the price; I thought that I must have misheard.

"Two pounds."

Two pounds? Two pounds!

It was a preposterous amount. Two pence perhaps. I was prepared to pay two pence. But two pounds. I mean, two pounds!

I turned to my dad, who was standing behind me; I could already feel my bottom lip begin to quiver; felt the first hint of wetness at the corner of my eye.

"It's too much, I'm afraid, son."

And I knew that he was right. It was too much.

It was a lesson. In commerce. In book collecting. Ultimately, in pragmatism.

Reading #5: *Biggles Goes to War*

Although it may sound as though this is going to be another story of Biggles' exploits during the First World War, *Biggles Goes to War* (Oxford University Press, 1938) recounts an episode in Biggles' life during the inter-war years.

Biggles is requested to come to the aid of a small Eastern European nation, which is being threatened by a larger neighbour. The names that W. E. Johns gives to the two nations concerned are fictional—Maltovia and Lovitzna, with capital cities of Janovica and Shavros respectively—but from his description of their geography, it would appear that he is imagining the current country of Ukraine split into two halves along a border formed by the Dnieper—or Dnipro—River: "Maltovia is a principality lying slightly to the north-east of the Black Sea." (p. 14); "'The Nieper is in Lovitzna."—'I know, but only just, and it runs parallel with the frontier."' (p. 105).

Re-reading the book in May 2022, three months after Russia's invasion of Ukraine, which threatens to divide a country roughly on the lines suggested by Johns, there is a grim impression of life imitating fiction.

It is interesting to note that in a desire to help the underdog, Biggles is prepared to commit a crime. The Foreign Enlistment Acts of 1819 and 1870 make it unlawful for a British subject to join the armed forces of any state warring with another state at peace with Britain, but Biggles states that: "…we shall be proud to wear our Maltovian uniforms." (p. 30). Although he is adopting the role of a 'gun for hire' or mercenary, he assuages his conscience by believing himself to be a knight errant; a description that attaches to it more highly-regarded notions of chivalry and honour. In this 'guise, Biggles is even prepared to break international aviation law; the very same law for which he is later employed to act as custodian during his stint working for Scotland Yard: "'We all know that by making an unauthorised landing at Weisheim, instead of landing at an official customs airport, we are committing a breach of international regulations punishable by imprisonment; that is a risk we must be prepared to take." (p. 26). However, once committed to the enterprise, Biggles is not someone to leave a job unfinished: "'Duty to those we serve and finishing the job we start on.'" (p. 147). It is a powerful rallying cry. *Biggles Goes to War* was published in May 1938. The *Anschluss*—or the annexation of Austria into Nazi Germany—had occurred on 12 March of the same year, and the Munich Agreement, which was signed by Germany, the United Kingdom, France and Italy, and which permitted cession to Germany areas of northern and western Bohemia and northern Moravia—known in Germany as the *Sudetenland*—was signed on 30 September. The Agreement was also known as the Munich Betrayal, and it would be interesting to know how Johns regarded the treaty. Perhaps if he disagreed with Neville Chamberlain's apparent appeasement towards Hitler's government, he reconciled that Biggles' unlawful stance in trying to make a stand against a threatening bully was justified?

At the conclusion of *Biggles Goes to War*, Biggles finds a solution to the conflict between Maltovia and Lovitzna by bringing about conditions whereby a peace can be negotiated between the two sides before the League of Nations in Geneva.

It is interesting to see, that in fiction, one man is capable of ending a war. Sadly, the reality of the current conflict in Ukraine also shows that one man is capable of starting one.

The Victor's Truth

According to President Vladimir Putin there is no war happening in Ukraine. The offensive that Russia launched against that country, which started on 24 February 2022 is simply a 'special military operation'. Similarly, former-President of the United States of America, Donald Trump denies inciting his supporters to storm Congress on 6 January 2021. To me, what is happening in Ukraine looks like a war; and what happened on the steps of the Capitol building looked like a provoked insurrection. So, what is the truth?

I am not a philosopher, and neither is Biggles. Indeed, Biggles does not even claim to be a politician: "Biggles laughed scornfully. 'Me, a politician? Not on your life! I'm a soldier.'" (*Biggles Goes to War*, p. 253). I will leave discussions on whether Truth is relative or absolute to those better qualified to answer them. When you have Plato's views on the topic lining up in direct opposition to Nietzsche, who are you going to believe? However, for myself, I think that the Correspondence Theory of Truth contains a definition, which is useful to adhere to for day-to-day living: Truth is determined only by how it relates to the world and whether it accurately corresponds to that world. So, I would still argue that what is happening in Ukraine *corresponds* to a war, and what happened on the steps of the Capitol building *corresponded* to a provoked insurrection.

Fake news is a weapon not solely restricted to the governments of Russia or the US, and appears to have mushroomed since the advent of social media. We live in an Age when a sensationalist Lie is more commercially valuable than a dull Truth. However, as a phenomenon in itself, fake news is nothing new.

One of the most enduring mysteries in British history is the fate of the Princes in the Tower. The two young sons of King Edward IV, Edward, Prince of Wales and Richard, Duke of York were last seen in the Tower of London in 1483, and their subsequent disappearance has never been satisfyingly explained. Popular school textbooks—certainly the ones that I would have first read during History lessons at around the same time that I read *Biggles Goes to War*—all point the finger of blame at the Princes' uncle, Richard III. It was held that Richard did away with his two nephews in order to leave the way to the throne unchallenged for himself. The image of a wicked Richard, hunchbacked and ambitious for power, has been the popular impression for centuries, mainly thanks to the eponymous play by William Shakespeare and the long-standing biography by Thomas More. However, there also exists an entirely different interpretation of the events in the Tower; one that is convincingly expounded by Josephine Tey in her book *The Daughter of Time*. She argues that Richard III had no reason to kill the Princes in order to ascend to the throne; his rule was already secured by the document *Titulus Regius*, which had been confirmed by Parliament. On the other hand, his successor, Henry VII, had no such direct right of ascendancy and, for him, the young Princes would have represented a direct threat to his ambitions of ruling the country. But this is not something that is mentioned in school history books. There, the facts are black and white: Richard III is bad; Henry VII is good. The reason. It is the victor who writes the histories. Henry defeated Richard III at the Battle of Bosworth Field on 22 August 1485, heralding the end of the Plantagenet era and the start of the Tudor one. Richard's subsequent chroniclers––Shakespeare; More—were products of the Tudor Age, writing from a viewpoint, which was going to be necessarily skewed. During the intervening centuries, odd historians have put forward a case for Richard's innocence, but it has not been until recent times, more than five hundred years after his death, that a momentum has grown in Richard's favour.

In *Biggles Goes to War*, Biggles describes some of the qualities that he believes characterise the English as: "…a love of justice, a sense of right and wrong, and sympathy for the under-dog." (*Biggles Goes to War*, p. 30). Richard III has been the underdog of history for almost half a millennium, but it is just possible that some of the fake news, which might have wronged him in the past will be popularly overturned such that his reputation is restored and justice finally served. Putin and Trump might both take note.

Reading #6: *Biggles in the South Seas*

Fifteen years after first reading *Biggles in the South Seas*, I found myself in French Polynesia, travelling between the islands of Tahiti, Moorea, Raiatea, Huahine, Bora Bora and Maupiti. Was my early reading of *Biggles in the South Seas* an inspiration for my travel? Undoubtedly. Admittedly, there had been other influences, too—Willard Price's *South Sea Adventure* and the various accounts of the Mutiny on the Bounty, when I had been a child; and the novels of Jack London and Herman Melville, and the *South Sea Tales* by Robert Louis Stevenson, when I was older. Gauguin's paintings? Not such a motivation; not a fan.

For me, the Society Islands of the South Pacific represented somewhere about as far-flung from my home as I could possibly find; tiny specks of land cast adrift upon a vast ocean of water. I think that Biggles was similarly struck by their sense of isolation; an isolation that was only penetrated by the advent of the airplane, as he comments: "This place is certainly the end of the world." (p. 90).

My first point of entry to the islands was very late one night, arriving into the darkness of Fa'a'ā International Airport in Papeete in the early-summer of 1992—Andre Agassi was soon to win Wimbledon and *Take That* were about to burst into the pop charts, but neither of those monumental world events stirred the slightest ripple of interest in my new island home. My first impression of Papeete was of a bustling hotchpotch; a cosmopolitan port city, acting as a crossroads for many travellers and nationalities, largely unchanged from the time when Biggles landed there: "There were a few well-dressed tourists, mostly Americans, brawny island skippers, bearded down-at-heel white men of many nationalities, half-castes of every shade between black and yellow, Chinese traders, and good-looking Polynesians, some with hibiscus or other tropical blossoms tucked behind their ears or into their hair." (p. 40). The one oasis of calm—and cool–—was the Post Office, whose trade revolved more around selling rare stamps to collectors than it did distributing any mail.

For as long as I can remember I have had a fascination with islands: their remoteness; their aspect of self-containment; often, simply, their smallness. In a vast world, even in a vast country, an island can often represent an area of land, which is more quantifiable to the human mind: its borders are obvious and undisputed; its limits exposed and known. The islands that Biggles ventured to in *Biggles in the South Seas* were more remote and more inaccessible than any that I ever visited. His sights were set on the Tuamotus and ultimately the Marquesas, one thousand kilometres' distance from Papeete. Where many of the islands of Polynesia are the classic 'desert islands' of popular imagination—low-lying coral atolls; sandy beaches; swaying palm trees—the Marquesas are an entirely different proposition: "…being volcanic rock covered with jungle… all jumbled up with mountains thousands of feet high." (p. 22). There is a paradox here: the islands of paradise and the islands of hell, and Biggles was to encounter both during his sojourn in the South Pacific: "The only word that he could find to describe it was 'fairyland'. What impressed him most was the transparent blueness of the crystal-clear atmosphere and the delicate blue of the sky in contrast to the emerald green of the palms and deep clear turquoise of the water, through which swam hundreds of fish, some large, of every colour of the rainbow." (p. 88); compared to "Biggles had seen many jungles, but never growth so impenetrable as that which fringed the creek… their faces were soon covered with spots of blood from the vicious bites of sandflies…and even if they did not wander into a swamp as deadly as quicksand, which was probable, they would certainly lose their way in the darkness." (pp 194-196). However, W. E. Johns acknowledges that condition popularly known as 'island fever', and of which I fear I have caught a chronic dose: "You'll come back.

Once you have been to the Islands you can't ever forget them, and one day they will call you back." (p. 254). I haven't returned to the Society Islands since that time, but other islands have called me since. That's one of the things about islands: there are just so many of them! Why would you return, when there are so many others out there waiting to be explored? And, whereas when I travelled through French Polynesia, I travelled alone, I find myself travelling through *Biggles in the South Seas* escorted by a companion: Mildred. And, despite a recurring theme of 'girl power' throughout the novel (see *Mary Anning and Joan Worralson*), I fear that Mildred's monofocus will leave her unimpressed by the wonder and the beauty of the natural surroundings, and will home in on a couple of instances of the N-word and several references to 'mop heads', to the exclusion of the wider picture. Or, is it me who is being myopic?

The Power of Humour

There is always a feeling of some kind of satisfaction when reading a book when it is possible to catch the author out in a mistake. I should know: priggish child that I was, I was always on the lookout for an opportunity to pit my knowledge against that of authority. Often, it would be facts that I had gleaned from the Biggles books, which would be my source of information, but sometimes… just sometimes, W. E. Johns would let me down and get his facts wrong.

In *Biggles' Second Case* (Hodder, 1948)—an excellent, thrilling story, by the way, reviewed later (see Reading #15: *Biggles' Second Case*)—Biggles is given an assignment, which takes him to the hugely remote Kerguelen islands, in the southern-most region of the Indian Ocean, close to the Antarctic. There, amidst the ice flows, Algy and Bertie spot: "…a quarter of a mile away two polar bears were swimming strongly towards another 'berg." (*Biggles' Second Case*, p. 90). Of course, every school-child knows that polar bears only live in the Arctic and not in the southern hemisphere. It was a rare opportunity for me to score a point over my mentor Johns. Another zoological subject, which found Johns habitually at sea was that of the giant squid, so much so that I have devoted an entire chapter to the topic (see *Feke, Feke!*).

Whilst feeling pride at being able to display the range of my childhood knowledge, I would have been better served to remember the wisdom of the old adage that 'pride comes before a fall'.

One day in my junior school class, our teacher asked what seemed like the easiest question in the world:

"How many sides has a circle?"

Little Johnny Keen's hand was one of the first up in the air.

"One, sir. The answer is one."

The teacher smiled at me sympathetically, before shaking his head; inviting other pupils to answer with the correct answer.

I stared in disbelief. I knew that the answer to the question was 'one'. I thought that the teacher must have misheard me. Johnny Keen persisted:

"Sir! Sir! The answer is one."

The teacher turned to me again; this time his expression less indulgent.

"I heard you the first time, Bradley. You are mistaken. Can anyone give me the correct answer?"

How could I be mistaken? Me, who knew that polar bears lived in the Arctic and that giant squid did not walk on land. Besides, a circle *did* have one side. It was a fact. It was incontrovertible. Thomas Gradgrind would back me up. I was prepared to risk the further ire of my teacher to stake my point. After all, if W. E. Johns could occasionally be mistaken, it was not beyond the bounds of possibility that my teacher might sometimes be mistaken, too.

I had my hand in the air again; a nascent "Sir!" already forming on my lips, when I was beaten to it by Billy Thick:

"The answer is two, sir."

The teacher beamed; pointed at the astonished child:

"Very good. The answer *is* two. And do you know what those two sides are?"

Billy Thick sank into his more customary silence; his knowledge exhausted. However, the teacher did not require an answer; the punchline of his joke was to be his, and his alone:

"A circle has two sides. An inside and an outside."

Upon which declaration he burst into peals of manic laughter.

Amidst the collective class hysteria that followed, I alone could feel tears prick the corners of my eyes. They were the same tears that had rolled at Arundel upon learning the price of *Biggles in the Gobi* (See *A Disappointment in Arundel*). They were tears of frustration; tears of humiliation. The tears of learning a hard lesson and paying a high price: humour can often trump wisdom, no matter how much you might think you know.

Feke, Feke!

There is one subject, which W. E. Johns returns to with surprising regularity, but where his research continually lets him down: this subject is the giant squid (*Architeuthis dux*).

References to giant squid occur in seven Biggles stories, albeit one very fleetingly. In the other six books, either Biggles or one of his companions manages to have a very close encounter with sometimes multiple giant squid; indeed, so frequent are Biggles' encounters that he should be considered something of a world expert. However, the descriptions of the squid that result from these sightings leave something to be desired, and reveal the lack of a trained scientific mind.

"It was a great grey slobbering mass the size of a barrage balloon—or it looked that size to me. The colour was elephant grey, and in fact, it might have been an enormous elephant without any legs." (*Biggles – Charter Pilot*, p.13); "A great, pig-like body as large as a barrel, with two long tentacles protruding in front and a number of shorter ones behind." (*Biggles, Air Commodore*, p.172); "In the bright moonlight he could now see tentacles plainly, two long ones, not less than twenty feet in length, held out in front, and a tangle of smaller ones." (*Biggles in Australia*, p.35); "Once, as the moonlight caught its eyes, Algy had to strangle an exclamation. They were white, flat, like tea plates." (*Biggles and the Deep Blue Sea*, p.51). So, put it all together and what have we got? An enormous grey slobbering body with two long tentacles in front and a mass of smaller tentacles behind and two large white eyes. Perhaps not so wide of the mark after all?

However, it is on the subject of the squid's behaviour and habitat where Biggles' accounts might be treated with dubiousness by the wider scientific community. Johns' most consistent error when describing the giant squid is to so often place the creature travelling on land. Although small octopuses will occasionally crawl across rocks to get from one water source to another or to ambush prey, the giant squid is usually a dweller of deep waters, typically temperate oceans rather than the tropical oceans where Johns places them, and they neither come onto land nor are capable of the overland speeds that Johns suggests: "Nearing the end of his run, a swift glance backward revealed both monsters not thirty yards behind, moving swiftly over the ground in a sort of rolling motion." (*Biggles, Air Commodore*, p.174); "The monster was overtaking Donald, and it seemed to me that nothing could save him." (*Biggles - Charter Pilot*, p.14); "'That fella no walk on rocks, eh?' asked Algy in dismay. 'Him walk pretty damn quick,' answered Tauri grimly." (*Biggles Flies Again*, p.90)

Little blame can be put on Johns, though, for his mistake: to this day, the giant squid remains a hugely elusive creature; the first video of a live specimen to be photographed in its natural environment only having been taken as recently as 2004. At the time that Johns was writing, the giant squid fell firmly into the category of sea monster, as much a creature of myth as of reality.

One report of a giant squid that Johns would have been aware of was the strange case involving the raft of the *SS Britannia*.

SS Britannia was a British passenger ship, which was sunk in the mid-Atlantic, 700 miles west of Freetown, Sierra Leone in 1941, by a German cruiser. Survivors took to lifeboats and rafts, many drifting for weeks before rescue. *The Illustrated London News* of 1 November 1941 ran a lively and well-publicised account of

Lieutenant R. E. G. Cox's survival on one such raft, entitled 'The Most Macabre Episode of the War at Sea: Marine Monsters Devour Men Adrift on a Raft'. The account was later included in Bernard Heuvelmans' book *In the Wake of the Sea-Serpents*, (Hart-Davis, 1968). The story records how the tiny raft was 'assailed by sharks and other marine monsters, which devoured men under the eyes of their comrades'. The account was accompanied by an illustration by Captain Bryan de Grineau, which depicts the perilous nature of life on the raft, floating above an ocean in which can be seen the fins of several circling sharks; a large manta ray; and, with its tentacles reaching out to pluck a man from the deck, what appears to be a giant squid. The story of the giant squid attack quickly became an urban myth of the Second World War, and could easily have further fuelled Johns' imagination on a subject that he had been writing about since 1934.

Despite it being apparent from his descriptions that it is the giant squid that Johns is writing about in the seven Biggles books, he very rarely uses the term 'giant squid' itself: "Twice he glided down towards the lagoon as if to land, but each time the giant squid moved sideways towards him and he knew that it was watching him." (*Biggles Flies Again*, p.90).

In *Biggles Flies Again* and *Biggles in the South Seas*, Johns most commonly talks about an octopus, although in *Biggles in the South Seas* he refers to the local Polynesian word for the creature: '*feke*'. Throughout the other books, the word that Johns most frequently uses is 'decapod', literally meaning something that is 'ten-footed'. Although this would appear to encompass the giant squid, the term is not accurate. Decapods are an order of crustaceans, which include crabs, lobsters and shrimps, whereas squid fall under the phylum Mollusca and are actually cephalopods. Johns only uses the term cephalopod once, in the last book in which he features the creature: "'I fancy it must be a decapod; the sort I believe is called a cephalopod. I've never seen a live one, but there's a model in the Oceanographic Museum in Monaco.'" (*Biggles and the Deep Blue Sea*, p.61)

Giant squid appear on the cover art and internal illustrations of several of the Biggles books, including several foreign language editions. These include covers for the first editions of *Biggles Flies Again* and *Biggles in Australia*; the *Boys' Friend Library* #630 of July 1938, which serialised *Biggles Flies Again*; the

Armada paperback edition of *Biggles in the South Seas*, which used as its influence the illustration from page 105 of the first edition of *Biggles in the South Seas*; *Biggles Reprend le Manche*, which is a French translation of *Biggles Flies Again*; and *Biggles a Temně Modré Moře*, which is a Czech translation of *Biggles and the Deep Blue Sea* published by Toužimský and Moravec of Prague.

Personally, I have always enjoyed Johns' depictions of giant squid; their lack of scientific accuracy is neither here nor there. The appearance of a giant squid in a Biggles books signifies an exciting encounter; a passage of thrilling text; a raising of the reader's heartbeat; and an excursion into the imagination. And surely this is everything that an encounter with a giant squid should be? Certainly, Johns' descriptions of the giant squid were sufficient inspiration to leave me with an eternal fascination for these magnificent and mysterious denizens of the deep.

Action Man: Deep Sea Diver

The pearl diving that is described in *Biggles in the South Seas* predates the advent of SCUBA (Self-Contained Underwater Breathing Apparatus) and modern forms of portable diving equipment by at least a decade, although a form of Aqua-Lung, invented by Gagnan and Cousteau, and which is considered the earliest diving regulator, had existed from the early 1940s. Before this time, the options for underwater exploration involved either holding your breath—a common practice amongst many indigenous communities and the reason why pearl diving was considered one of the most dangerous pursuits on the planet—or going down in a weighted air-tight outfit, linked up to an air compressor on board a surface vessel—as described in *Biggles in the South Seas*—and being a scarcely less perilous activity. Looking like a steampunk astronaut, the type of deep sea diving that W. E. Johns describes had barely advanced from Victorian times and the imagination of Jules Verne. But, for an adventurously-minded boy, there held its romantic appeal. The very nature of exploration required an element of danger and discomfort; the kind of activity that could only be undertaken by a man of action. And I happened to know just the fellow.

My Action Man was of Seventies vintage: gripping hands and realistic hair, but before eagle eyes. He even had a beard, which made him look even more macho, albeit faintly naval. He had a scar down one side of his face, which might be considered an over-compensation for his lack of any genital organs. The original outfit, which had accompanied my Action Man had been a simple soldier's kit—roll-neck sweater, trousers, beret and kit-bag, all in khaki—but my mum had supplemented his wardrobe by a succession of home-knits of varying sartorial success. The rough-stitch polar-neck had complemented his grizzled, outdoorsy vibe; the crocheted tank top had been more reminiscent of the Knight 'posed covers' (see *The Posed Photo Covers*) and had been rather more Hampstead Garden Suburb than Call of the Wild.

However, additional outfits soon arrived from an unexpected quarter. Answering a personalised advertisement card, which had been posted up in our local newsagent's window, my dad returned one day with a big box of second-hand Action Man paraphernalia, purchased from a house a couple of streets way. In a world before eBay, it is hard to remember the innocence of those times, when a personalised ad wasn't just for dating—6'2", GSOH and must enjoy travel, spicy food and country music—or to obtain the dubious services of Jenny, 38-24-36. When I searched through the box, I discovered a miscellaneous collection of IED-severed plastic limbs and a mismatch of half-complete outfits but, amidst all the debris of an Action Man outgrown, there was a treasure: a complete Deep Sea Diver outfit.

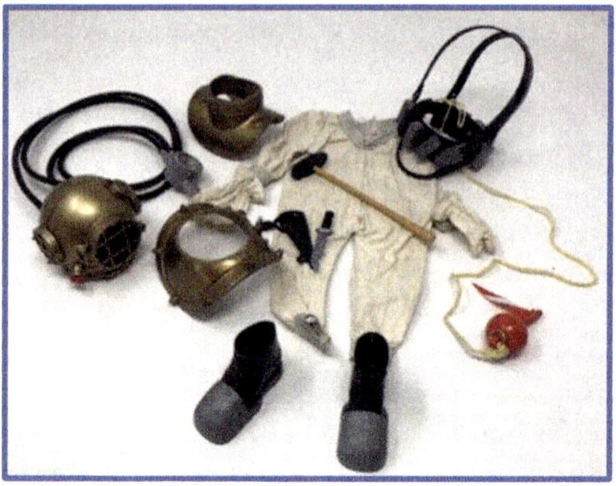

I can still remember the moment of first cladding my Action Man in this strange, otherworldy attire. There was an all-in-one, white boiler suit—bizarrely, not unlike the photo of Biggles on the front cover of *Biggles Forms a Syndicate* (see *The Posed Photo Covers*); big, bulky black boots, with detachable heavy, lead weighted caps—and they genuinely were heavy; quite possibly real lead in those days—and an enormous brass-coloured diver's helmet, which I pulled over my Action Man's head, so that only his eyes and bushy beard could be seen through the latticed visor. And then there were the accoutrements: a knife, which fitted into a sheath at his thigh; a hammer slung across his chest; and a long cable, with a pressure gauge attached, which looked rather like a doctor's stethoscope, and which provided his lifeline to a terra firma from which he would soon submerge. Even as a child, I was under no illusion that this kind of equipment was patently inadequate to tackle all the terrifying horrors of the deep. Whenever I dressed my Action Man in his deep-sea diver outfit, it was with a sense of trepidation, conscious that he might not return from the bottom of the bathtub or the depths of the garden pond, into which I had consigned him. It was always with a sense of relief when, mission accomplished, he would return to the surface and indulge in a spot of R&R wearing his home-knit tank top, or going *au naturel* once again.

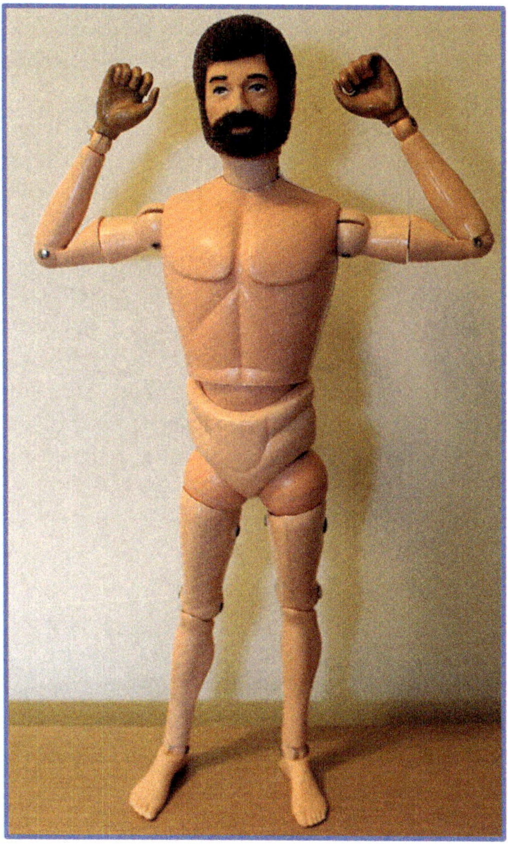

Giant Clams and Wet T-Shirts

There was a growing fascination with underwater exploration during the 1970s. A lot of this interest could have been put down to the long-running TV series by French explorer and film-maker Jacques Cousteau: *The Undersea World of Jacques Cousteau*. For me, a greater influence was less educational and more salacious: Peter Yates' 1977 filming of the Peter Benchley novel, *The Deep*.

The Deep starred Robert Shaw—fresh from *Jaws*, also written by Benchley and which was released two years earlier—Nick Nolte and Jacqueline Bisset, putting in a show-stealing performance in a tightly-clinging, white t-shirt.

Jacqueline Bisset's white t-shirt aside, one of the most memorable scenes in the movie is Bisset's character Gail Berke diving to explore a shipwreck, only to get her arm trapped by an unseen lurking sea creature hidden within the wreckage. Her oxygen is running out and she has nothing with which to free herself. Around the same time, there were plenty of urban myths circulating concerning giant clams and what parts of the anatomy various divers had managed to get stuck in them. The dull reality is that the adductor muscles in a giant clam, which it uses to close its shell, operate too slowly to take a swimmer by surprise, and no human deaths have ever been attributed to them. Nevertheless, the image of being trapped underwater is a powerful and an enduring one, particularly to the impressionable schoolboy that I was at the time.

And it was not just Jacqueline Bisset's giant clams—some euphemism clearly intended—which were memorable in *The Deep*. The film did for conger eels what *Jaws* had done for the great white shark, and it also introduced me to the concept of 'the bends', a hitherto unknown anxiety which had even more influence on me than the later, same-named album by Radiohead.

Properly known as decompression sickness, the bends occurs when divers experience rapid changes in pressure—as when surfacing too quickly—causing dissolved gases, mainly nitrogen, to form as bubbles in the body's tissues, with potentially fatal consequences. As a child, I am not quite sure when I ever thought that I might find myself in this kind of situation, but it added to a catalogue of ways in which it was possible to die, of which, previously, I had lived in ignorance. Nevertheless, I considered it a prudent policy to get out of the bath as slowly as possible, just to be on the safe side.

An early memory I have from schooldays, but it is a suspiciously vague one, too, is of being read a story by our teacher about two boys who swam into a long, underwater tunnel. Only one returned. It seems like rather a sadistic story to read to an innocently youthful audience but, maybe, it was meant to serve as a warning tale. In subsequent years, I have tried to trace the particular story. Without success.

In *Biggles in the South Seas*, Ginger and his two Polynesian friends, Full Moon and Shell-Breaker, discover an underwater cavern, which they swim down to, stretching Ginger's underwater endurance to its limits: "To say that he was frightened as he went through the gloomy entrance would be to put it mildly, but he set his teeth and swam on grimly behind the two figures which were gliding through the water in front of him, still beckoning." (*Biggles in the South Seas*, p. 123). Ginger reaches a point where he knows that he has swam too far such that to turn back is not an option; he can only carry on in the hope that he will reach the pocket of air that his companions have promised him.

It is a terrifying image. Possibly the origin-story of my memory about the two boys in the underwater tunnel? I am now aware of the power of false memory syndrome. How many of the events that we believed happened in our past are real, and how many are imaginary? Without concrete evidence, it is hard to be sure. Jacqueline Bisset and her white t-shirt. Surely, that is not a false memory, too? I may have to re-watch the entire film in order to find out.

Sink or Swim

It may be wondered why quite so many underwater situations would stick in the memory and hold such fascination—and, in some cases, such terror—for my younger self—*Biggles in the South Seas*; *The Deep*; Jacques Cousteau. Well, the simple fact of the matter was that, at the time, I couldn't swim.

School swimming lessons were a source of torment for me. Whilst the juvenile Mark Spitzes of my class were allowed to splash and play unsupervised in the town's large municipal swimming pool, the unlucky band of sinkers—we numbered five hapless individuals—were whisked away to a separate side-pool, given a hard, white rectangle of polystyrene, and forced to endure the embarrassment of trying to propel ourselves ten yards on top of the water without imitating stones. I was not so much scared of the water as I was of the shame. I simply couldn't understand my inability to float, even when clinging to the rectangle of polystyrene and kicking my feet like the most energetic Cossack dancer. Most other rite-of-passage activities I had mastered with some degree of fluency. Why was swimming proving to be quite so difficult?

I felt that there was an element of magic about the skill. It was not so much something that you learned; it was something that you could either do or you couldn't do, and it was a twinkle of fairy-dust that existed between the two opposite states. And, for some unfathomable reason, I inhabited the side, which had not yet had the magic wand of buoyancy waved over me.

In these circumstances, the reporting of any exploits, which occurred underwater were full of intrigue for me: they seemed full of dangers; undertaken by people who possessed skills, which set them apart from my own capabilities. I could not imagine either Biggles, Jacqueline Bisset or Jacques Cousteau appearing quite so effortlessly deft, if they had been encumbered by a white, polystyrene rectangle during their adventures.

In the end, my moment of enlightenment came during a family holiday. It was neither a magic wand, fairy dust, a white polystyrene rectangle or half-hour weekly humiliations in my local swimming pool that I needed in order to master the art of swimming, but one long intensive burst of activity, which I was fortunate enough to obtain on my first ever extended overseas holiday—a fortnight's stay in Gran Canaria, where the hotel that me and my mum and dad stayed in possessed a thirty-metre outside heated swimming pool. And, while my dad fought his own private battles with towels on sunbeds, I was able to splash and frolic in the water with a freedom that I had not enjoyed before and, suddenly, before I realised it, I was swimming, first widths, then lengths, and then multiple lengths. Perhaps a bit of fairy dust had landed on me somewhere after all.

It was just in time. The following autumn, I entered the first year of my secondary school, and there the teaching methods were harsher. The school was—wrongly—proud to possess its own unheated pool in the far corner of the grounds. In the winter, ice floated across the surface of the water and, year-round, a thin miasma of cold mist seemed to hover just above the surface of the uninviting soup. Here, the strategy was sink or swim, survival of the fittest; boys were pushed into the icy waters, regardless of swimming prowess or proficiency. Thankfully, I swam. But it was a close call.

Later, in Polynesia, I would be doubly grateful for the ability to swim. The coral reefs around Moorea and Bora Bora were wondrous pleasure-grounds to explore and, in Bora Bora, I was fortunate enough to swim in close proximity to blacktip reef sharks, leaving a hard, white rectangle of polystyrene to the consigns of distant memory.

The Best Things in Life are Free

It is reputed that Coco Chanel said that "The best things in life are free.". It is sometimes not added that she went on to say that "The second-best things are very, very expensive." Who is more likely to quote this well-known phrase: poor people or rich people?

In *Biggles in the South Seas*, Ginger is horrified when he sees the Polynesian girl, Full Moon, seduced by the cheap tat that is available in Lo Sing's store, when he considers her to be surrounded by far more wondrous natural treasures all around her, all of which are free: "She'll look like a French doll and stink like a chemist's shop for a couple of days, and kid herself that she's the cat's whisker. Then she'll go swimming and forget all about it." (*Biggles in the South Seas*, p. 118).

Certainly, for me, the things that I most enjoyed during the time I spent in Polynesia were all free—swimming in the lagoons of the beautiful atolls; seeing the amazing variety of colourful fish; climbing the high mountains; enjoying the lush, tropical landscape—but, perhaps like Ginger, it is easy to forget that it had also cost a hell of a lot of money in terms of an international airfare in order to be in a position to enjoy all this complimentary bounty.

During my first year of secondary school, we had a very strict Geography teacher called Mr Clayton. Now, Geography—thanks in no small part to Biggles—was one of my favourite subjects, so it was rare for me to be the object of Mr Clayton's wrath but, nevertheless, I had quickly decided that a policy of anonymity was the best way to survive his lessons. Looking back now, Mr Clayton must have been a rather progressive young teacher; at the time, he merely seemed angry and eccentric and distinctly elderly—pushing thirty, at least. Before the start of every lesson, Mr Clayton would demand the class be silent and would then take us through a five-minute exercise of Zen-like meditation. Not that any of us boys had ever heard of Zen or meditation back then; the ritual was simply explained away as one of Mr Clayton "little eccentricities".

"Close your eyes. Breathe deeply. Feel the weight of your body on the chair. Listen to the most distant sound," so Mr

Clayton would slowly intone. And, as a class, we obeyed; fear quelling any nascent sedition.

One day, Mr Clayton entered the classroom looking more cheerful than was his norm. He was smiling; positively beaming. It was rather alarming; it seemed to spell trouble ahead for someone. We were still taken through our usual five-minute round of meditation but, then, instead of telling us to open our Geography textbooks and start reading, Mr Clayton posed a question to the class:

"What is the meaning of life?"

It is a question that has stumped sages and philosophers across the Ages, so, given such a track record of failure, no reason why a suburban classroom of eleven-year-olds shouldn't have a stab at finding a solution.

Ahead of the rest of us, a couple of desks removed from me, a contemporary, Greenan, had his hand in the air, confident that he had the answer.

"Yes, Greenan."

"To make money, sir."

The benevolent expression on Mr Clayton's face changed instantly. It was obvious that the trouble, which had been predicted was about to arrive, and it was going to be Greenan who would face the full force of it. However, before any reckoning was forthcoming, Mr Clayton had turned his attention on another hapless victim:

"Yes, Dunbar."

Dunbar?

I had only been semi-conscious that I had had my hand up in the air; the limb seemed to be operating of its own volition; totally separated, body from mind. Nevertheless, some uncontrolled force was operating my mind, too, and a signal, which originated there was sufficient to have the following words expel from my mouth:

"To be happy, sir."

There were sniggers from some corners of the room; nervous chuckles, which indicated that most of the class thought that I would soon be joining Greenan in whatever retribution awaited us.

Instead, the ghost of a smile returned to Mr Clayton's face. He never acknowledged whether my answer was the one that he had been expecting; instead he simply said:

"Open your textbooks. Start reading from page seventy-five."

Several days later, I learned through the school gossip-mill, that Mr Clayton had recently become a new father.

Now, I am a father myself. Not with any overt philosophy in mind, but I have tended to try to give my own son experiences over possessions. Spiritual worth over material goods. Does it make him happy? Poor little bugger, it probably just means there is nothing concrete for him to inherit when I peg it.

Except for a very fine collection of Biggles books.

Reading #7: *Biggles & Co.*

An unusual instance of Biggles being propelled into the world of money and commerce occurs in *Biggles & Co.* (Oxford, 1936). Usually, Biggles acts out of the most altruistic of intentions and, although he is always mindful of how he is going to fund any given operation, which might involve him in purchasing an aircraft, or buying sufficient supplies of fuel and food to transport him to the other side of the world, he is seldom brought up so close to the world of commerce; and a dirty world it can sometimes prove to be: "Large sums of money are at stake between men who are utterly unscrupulous… Twentieth century infidels who worship the golden calf." (p. 26). In setting up the business of Biggles & Co., Biggles takes on these money-loving infidels at their own game and, while the greedy and the unscrupulous come a cropper, Biggles is unabashed to claim his own, rightfully-earned, financial reward at the novel's conclusion: "There is a little matter of a cheque for fifteen thousand pounds which you promised… We may be airmen, but that doesn't mean that we can live on air." (p. 256). The noble exploits of a Robin Hood might be all well and good for legend but, back in the real world, there is food to be bought and bills to be paid; that nice, fancy Bentley, which Biggles owns, is not going to run itself.

Biggles & Co. is an early forerunner of how Biggles will find employment in his later career, fighting crime as a detective employed by Scotland Yard. Already here, we learn that his immediate superior Colonel Raymond, who was Biggles' Wing Intelligence Officer during the First World War, has just been made Assistant Commissioner of Police, and it is through the recommendations of Raymond that Biggles finds himself propelled into many of his subsequent adventures. However, before this period of Biggles' career can properly begin, global events intervene. Another world war is on the horizon, and there are signs of the suspicion and instability that was growing in Europe in *Biggles & Co.* The novel first appeared in serial form in *The Modern Boy* under the title *The Gold Flyers* in January 1936 and then as a book in April of the same year, three years prior to the outbreak of the Second World War. It is Algy, landing in Germany, close to the border with France, who describes the atmosphere: "A hush, almost sinister in its intensity, hung over the place, and endowed it with an atmosphere of cold hostility." (p. 115). Two months after *The Gold Flyers* was published, German troops re-occupied the Rhineland, a de-militarised zone running between France, Belgium and Germany, as designated by the Treaty of Versailles.

When Biggles and Ginger follow in Algy's footsteps, they discover an armed militia of troops wearing green uniforms and carrying guns. And someone else. An unexpected arrival from the past; the second manifestation of Biggles' arch-enemy Erich von Stalhein, in an appearance that firmly places him in the role of serial-baddie.

Von Stalhein is no cartoon-villain, though. His is a multifaceted character, making him a worthy adversary for Biggles. Within his own ideology, he exhibits many of the qualities that Biggles most admires: intelligence; courage; resourcefulness; honour. Perhaps what he lacks is an ability to act outside the rules, a crucial factor, which often allows Biggles to get the deciding hand over him.

Von Stalhein may be no cartoon-villain, but there is one element of cartoon-like humour in *Biggles & Co.* It is an episode, which brings to mind a scene from *Four Weddings and a Funeral*, where Hugh Grant is trapped in a small cupboard having to overhear Sophie Thompson and David Haig consummate their marriage: "He had just time to step back into the doorway behind him when several people walked into the room… but to his horrified surprise he saw that he was in nothing more than an alcove from which there was no exit." (p. 171).

A Nice Little Earner

My steadily burgeoning collection of Biggles books was short of one crucial factor: money. As I had discovered to my cost in Arundel (see *A Disappointment in Arundel*), if I hoped to acquire some of the Biggles titles that were not available to me in paperback, I was going to have to be prepared to stump up sums beyond the scope of my weekly pocket money. There was only one thing for it: I needed to get a job.

For someone not yet in their teens, the opportunities for gainful employment were rather limited, as I was soon to discover. There was the classic paper-round, but I was not a particularly early-riser; some of my friends seem to sell lottery tickets for the local football club, but it was something of a cartel, and I could not find my way inside of it. In the end, salvation once again appeared in the shape of a postcard in the local newsagent's window. This one was not advertising second-hand Action Man gear for sale, but was seeking people to deliver leaflets door-to-door for cash. For cash. I needed no more persuasion.

The first batch of leaflets turned up the following week. They arrived in several large boxes, which I stowed in my dad's garage. I was given my 'territory' and instructed that I should attempt to deliver them all by the same time next week. Beyond that I could please myself as to precisely how I went about the task. My 'territory' was a grid of a dozen or so streets, relatively close to my home. I set off walking; a rucksack containing as many leaflets as I could carry strapped to my back. Had I but known it, I was an early forerunner of Deliveroo and the gig economy. It was a pleasant-enough occupation. There was a novelty in the work for me, and the incentive of knowing that there was payment—in cash—at the end of it. Most boys are quite content given a routine—no matter how dull that routine may be—and I soon fitted my delivery job into the structure of my established schedule of home and school. I delivered when the weather was fair; I didn't deliver when the rain was pouring. I quickly worked out which houses had yappy dogs, which would jump up and try to bite the fingers of anyone unwary enough to stick them through a letterbox, and those houses I excluded from my round. I rocketed along the streets where the houses had short front drives or, better still, fronted directly onto the pavement; and I found time drag interminably along the leafy, affluent avenues, where the front drives stretched to a distant horizon.

Sometimes, I would be given several leaflets to deliver all at the same time, rather than just a single one and, although it meant carrying more weight, it also meant that I got paid an additional bonus. Sometimes, there were not just leaflets to deliver but free samples, too. On one memorable occasion, my dad's garage was piled high with countless boxes of tea bags, which I had to distribute to an unsuspecting neighbourhood.

I was fairly sure that my employer had local spies who reported back whether they had received their leaflets, or not, but I was a conscientious worker and—yappy dog houses notwithstanding—more of my leaflets found their intended markets than were ever dumped behind hedges.

And the money flowed in. Where I had only ever had a balance credited to my name in the sum of pence, all of a sudden there was a column for pounds added to the front of it. I had enough money to go back to the bookshop in Arundel and buy that copy of *Biggles in the Gobi* for £2 if I so chose to (see *A Disappointment in Arundel*).

But a Dunbar does not quickly forget. Once slighted, he holds a grudge for a long time, and I wouldn't allow that exorbitant bookseller who had made me cry the satisfaction of having my hard-earned money if it was the last copy of *Biggles in the Gobi* in the whole world.

Reading #8: *Biggles Flies West*

Sometimes all you want from a book is good, old-fashioned, uncomplicated entertainment, and *Biggles Flies West* provides it in bucket-loads. In fact, this should be a basic requirement of far more books.

The design of the first edition of *Biggles Flies West* is unique for books in the Oxford series, having dark blue boards, embossed on the front with the impression of a golden *onza* doubloon. The book also contains a photographic plate of the same doubloon and a silver 'Piece of Eight', both coins being ones in the possession of the author.

It would seem likely that these two coins provided the inspiration for W. E. Johns to write *Biggles Flies West*, which involves a classic treasure hunt among the islands of the Caribbean and the region previously known as the Spanish Main; a territory once the haunt of buccaneers and pirates, and classic tales of both adventure and skulduggery. Indeed, Johns makes several references to what is perhaps the most famous of all fictional accounts of piracy: Robert Louis Stevenson's *Treasure Island*: "'When I read *Treasure Island* at school I never thought the day would come when I'd be on one myself.'" (p. 181), with Biggles and his companions even adopting the roles of some of the characters from that book: "'Dick here is Jim Hawkins, Algy is Squire Trelawny, Ginger is Doctor Livesay, and I'm–'—'Captain Smollett,' put in Dick promptly." (p. 181).

Typical with many Biggles books, though, Johns also manages to include a great swathe of factual information about his subject, too, providing a veritable history lesson regarding the succession of English kings and queens: "The years rolled on. William the Fourth, Victoria, King Edward—the seventh of the name—King George the Fifth, the eighth King Edward, all ruled in turn, but still the island kept its secret." (p. 28), and, of course, a background of the history of piracy: "'Another colony sprang up at Port Royal, in Jamaica, which must have been a pretty hot spot… The old buccaneering business was forgotten and the one-time buccaneers became pirates pure and simple.'" (p. 51). We even get a lesson on language and etymology thrown in free for good measure: "'They called the stuff *boucan*, which was really the French word for cured beef. So they became known as *boucaniers* or, in our language, buccaneers.'" (p. 50).

A further trope within the book is Samuel Taylor Coleridge's *The Rime of the Ancient Mariner.* Algy directly quotes from the poem: "'A painted ship upon a painted ocean.'" (p. 232), but a more recognisable allusion is with the regular appearance of a large, white albatross in *Biggles Flies West*, usually coinciding with a death or a moment of danger: "There was a splintering crash as the bird struck the machine… The roar of the engines ceased abruptly." (p. 118). The albatross has long been considered a portentous symbol for mariners, and killing one a sign of ill omen. In *The Rime of the Ancient Mariner*, the narrator kills an albatross with a crossbow and is forced by his crew to wear the dead bird around his neck to display his guilt. In *Biggles Flies West*, the albatross is a bird slightly out of place. Not such an anomaly as the polar bear in *Biggles' Second Case*, and although there are occasional sightings in the Caribbean, the range of the albatross is more typically the wide oceans of the southern hemisphere, as is the case in *The Rime of the Ancient Mariner*, where the bird is spotted close to the Antarctic.

For me, there is an additional literary influence within *Biggles Flies West*: Charles Dickens. The start of the novel, set in a wretchedly poor, run down wharf of tenements and warehouses alongside the Thames in Wapping, reads much like a description of Dickens' Victorian London. I could imagine Oliver Twist or David Copperfield stepping out of the shadows when, in fact, the person to appear is Dick Denver.

Where Ginger had filled the role of the youthful protégé since his introduction in *The Black Peril*, his subsequent maturity into a fully qualified pilot at the start of *Biggles Hits the Trail* had left a vacancy for a naïve and unworldly asker-of-questions which, in *Biggles Flies West*, Dick is only too able and willing to fulfil. However, if Johns had hoped to introduce Dick as a fellow youth that his adolescent readers could recognise and empathise with, he certainly puts the poor lad—and, subsequently, his readers—through the mill. The violent loss of a parent; a vividly described near-death experience by drowning; and a close-call from having his throat cut by a razor-wielding ruffian not being the sum total of the misadventures that Dick must endure before the book reaches its thrilling conclusion.

And would Mildred agree with me regarding that 'thrilling conclusion'? I fear that she might have become sufficiently distracted along the way by three occurrences of the N-word, one 'tinpot' (p. 90), and an, admittedly, highly dubious discussion regarding racial purity in Central America to have ever reached that point in the book. Her loss? We are still a long way from truth and reconciliation.

Don't Take Careers Advice from Novels (or Computers)

The list of jobs that most boys want to do when they grow up is long and varied but, for many, it will have included such noble aspirations as to be a footballer, or train driver, or explorer, or astronaut. Nowadays, the slightly less noble YouTuber or influencer might also be added to the list. Sometimes these ambitions are fleeting, for others they endure; for a few, they are achieved. For me, I am sure that at some stage, I toyed with the idea of becoming a pirate: a fantasy that Biggles was able to briefly live out in *Biggles Flies West*: "'By thunder! Israel Hands himself!' he gasped. 'All we need is a Jolly Roger to fly at the peak and we should look as bonny a bunch of pirates as ever boarded a prize or sacked a town.'" (*Biggles Flies West*, p. 176). More lasting, though, was a slightly bizarre ambition to be a tramp. And the source of this ambition was not any of the Biggles books but, instead, the William books of Richmal Crompton, most specifically, *William and the Tramp*. The tramps of Richmal Crompton's imagination were not the unfortunate rough-sleepers of our urban city centres; they cut more romantic figures, slightly roguish, travelling the highways and byways of a beautiful English countryside, living on their wits, not constrained by society and convention. It was an appealing image to an idealist youngster.

I mentioned this ambition to my career's teacher at my secondary school who, not surprisingly, scoffed at the notion. He scoffed in exactly the same way when I later told him that I had decided to be a literary agent, so there is perhaps not too much to be drawn from the reaction. I am sure that I would have been met with exactly the same response if I had mentioned some of the jobs that I actually went on to do. At the time, careers advice was something of an oxymoron. It was the early 1980s and the country was in one of the worst recessions since the end of the Second World War. Jobs were in scarce supply and unemployment at record levels.

Into this adverse employment environment, my school started trialling a relatively new computer database of occupational information, called CASCAid (Careers Advisory Service Computer

Aid). The principles of the computer programme appeared simple enough. Each pupil filled out a long and detailed questionnaire about themselves, including interests and hobbies, favourite academic subjects, hopes and ambitions, and then all this data was entered into the computer with the objective being that the computer would advise you what job you were most suited to, based on your answers. So far, so good.

In my imagination, I have since transposed a huge, tape-rolling, paper-whirring, comic-book machine for the reality, which was merely being handed a very small slip of paper, like a fortune cookie, with the job title 'Home Office Cartographer' printed on it. It was something of an anti-climax. Like 'misogynist' (see *Biggles is Bad?*), I had to look up what a 'cartographer' actually did. It turned out to be someone who drew maps. It wasn't a footballer, or a train driver, or a pirate, or even a tramp, but it didn't sound too bad, all things considered. And, given the then parlous state of the economy, it was a case of beggars can't be choosers. If 'the computer says' that Home Office Cartographer was to be my destiny, who was I to disagree.

In the end, upon leaving school, working in a bookshop and serving angry women who wanted to burn Biggles books proved to be my immediate destiny. However, many years later, and remembering the computer's prediction, I did write to the Home Office, enquiring about possible employment as a Home Office Cartographer. I received a swift response from their Correspondence Section, thanking me for my enquiry, but going on to say: "The Home Office does not employ cartographers but if it is any help to you vacancies and general recruitment information can be found on the Home Office website."

'X' Marks the Spot

Although CASCAid may not have predicted the direction of my future career when they suggested that I should become a Home Office Cartographer, they were completely right about one thing: I do like maps.

As a child, I would spend hours tracing out the outlines of imaginary lands and then populating them with a topographical landscape of hills and rivers and trees; adding to this castles and towns and farms and, finally, little stick people. The size of my maps grew in direct proportion to the size of my ambition and the size of my imagination and, having quickly exhausted the limitations of the A4 sheet, and even run on beyond the possibilities of several A4 sheets joined together by Sellotape, I recognised the potential of rolls of wallpaper. Fortunately, my dad was a keen DIYer, and was often engaged in decorating one or other of the rooms in our house, and so spare rolls of wallpaper proved to be relatively easy to acquire for my own empire-building ambitions. Because, that was what these juvenile maps represented. They were the low-tech forerunner of Minecraft. My own imaginary world made real, laid out on the back of a roll of woodchip spread across the lounge carpet.

I'd forgotten all about this strange childhood obsession, until one day, completely by chance, I bumped into the girl—now a woman—that I used to sit next to in junior school on a commuter train, coming home from work. After the initial pleasantries and reintroductions, she suddenly said:

"Whatever happened to all those funny pictures you used to draw?"

Yes, whatever *did* happen to them? Where did all those imaginary realms end up? All those long rolls of wallpaper that harboured secret universes on their reverse. Perhaps like some undiscovered Van Gogh hidden beneath the brush strokes of a later artist, my juvenile cartography is pasted up on the walls of some unsuspecting householder's front room, only to be revealed when the paper peels, or fashions change, and they make a decision to redecorate. Too fanciful? Perhaps not. I was recently reminiscing with an old friend from my secondary school days about a story that we had written together during our first-year

English class when we had been eleven. Our class teacher, operating a system of discipline inspired by Evelyn Waugh's Paul Pennyfeather—"There will be a prize of half a crown for the longest essay, irrespective of any possible merit." (*Decline and Fall*)––had instructed our form to write a story on any subject, over the span of an entire term's length of lessons. Unabashedly plagiarising from Tolkien, our story recorded the adventures of a hobbit-like creature who found himself transported to a futuristic, space-age environment. The story was enlivened by the benefit of copious illustrations, and ran over the course of several exercise books. Many exercise books. This time, it was my turn to ask:

"Whatever happened to all those exercise books?"

"Oh, they're all up in the attic of my mum and dad's house. They never throw anything away."

A map plays a crucial role in *Biggles Flies West*. It is a classic treasure map, with 'X' marking the spot of the buried bounty. A picture of the map itself is recorded amongst the illustrations in the book. This particular map is quite crudely drawn, but it still records sufficient salient features to make it understandable. It depicts a small island, with areas of mangroves, hills, rocks and lagoon all marked, and a hastily sketched north-south axis to add authenticity. And, for all its basic design, it still has the capacity to stir the imagination. It makes the reader speculate as to the navigability of the lagoon; how impenetrable are the mangroves; what lies on the little islet in the far northeast corner?

A map in a book produces a small, self-contained world. A world the size of the novel, or the story. It has impenetrable boundaries formed by the page edges; there is no suggestion that there is any sentient existence beyond the limits of its extent; no 'Here be dragons' outside those that exist within the author's mind.

No One Ejaculates Like They Used to Do

Something that I never noticed when reading Biggles as a child, but which I find I can't help but be aware of now, is that Biggles ejaculates a lot. Practically in every book. No matter where he is, or what he's doing, he always finds time for a swift ejaculation, as in *Biggles Flies West*: "A low whistle left his lips. 'Oh-ho! Oh-ho!' he ejaculated quickly." (p. 48), or in *Biggles in the Jungle*: "'Great Scott!' he ejaculated for Ginger's benefit." (p. 38), or in *Biggles & Co.*: "Biggles started. 'Raymond, eh?' he ejaculated." (p. 10). In the same book, Biggles behaviour is such for Police Detective Boulanger to take him to one side and comment: "So you—how do you say?—pulled him off again, eh?'" (pp. 78-79); and, in *Biggles Defies the Swastika,* it is Biggles who finds himself on the wrong end of an innuendo: "He might not have seen the sailors had not one of them deliberately exposed himself." (p. 77).

Of course, over time, many words fall out of favour; some to disappear entirely from our popular vocabulary; others to change their common meaning, as is the case with 'ejaculates'.

Perhaps the most common phrases, which appear rather quaint and dated reading Biggles today are the oaths. Whenever either Biggles or one of his companions finds themselves in a tight spot, they invariably pepper their language with a few colourful expletives of the day: "Crikey!" (p. 113); "Fiddlesticks!" (p.39); "Great Scott!" (p. 185); even the occasional "Holy smoke!" (p. 193). Compared to most modern swear words, Biggles' language would appear commendably restrained and somewhat innocent.

It says a lot more about me than it does about W. E. Johns, but there is one passage of text which, for me, conjures up something far from innocent. I simply can't shake off the horrifying private image, which comes into my mind every time I read the sentence: "Full Moon and Shell-Breaker were recounting their adventures to an ejaculating circle of warriors." (*Biggles in the South Seas*, p. 247).

Reading #9: *Biggles in the Orient*

As my Biggles chronology approaches the Second World War, it may seem like rather a strange decision to come to one of the last of W. E. Johns' wartime books first. In the front pages of the book itself, publishers Hodder record that *Biggles in the Orient* was first published in November 1944 although, due to paper shortages, the book actually never saw the light of day until April 1945, only a month before VE Day, and four months before VJ Day. The book takes Biggles to the eastern theatre of the War, fighting against the Japanese in what was then Burma, and the book involves a lot of descriptions of flying and of aircraft, both of which were less in abundance in *Biggles Flies West.* So, we get a roll-call of some of the more popular British fighting aircraft of their day: "There's a Wimpey, a Beaufighter, a Mosquito, three Hurricanes, three Spits and a Typhoon." (p. 31). Which translate as the Vickers Wellington, the Bristol Beaufighter, the de Havilland Mosquito, the Hawker Hurricane, the Supermarine Spitfire, and the Hawker Typhoon. For good measure, W. E. Johns includes a couple of Japanese planes, too: "Once, a flight of three Mitsubishi bombers droned overhead on a westerly course; a little later six Zero fighters, flying at a great height, passed over, heading in the same direction, towards India." (p. 66).

Where Johns uses slang terms in *Biggles in the Orient*, such as in the case of calling a Wellington bomber a 'Wimpey', he provides a useful glossary of terms at the front of the book. This glossary includes words, which would have been typically spoken by airmen of the day, but which might be unfamiliar to a wider—predominately, younger—reading public. Many of these phrases have subsequently become part of popular speech, like 'browned off' for feeling bored or fed up; or 'a slice of cake' meaning that something is easy. Others have interesting, and often disputed derivations, such as the phrase 'Gone for a Burton', meaning that someone has died. It has been suggested that the expression is a play on the word 'bier', which is a stretcher, often used for carrying the dead and wounded. However, in German the word 'bier' means 'beer'. Burton Ale is a dark beer, named after the town Burton-on-Trent in Staffordshire, and it was suggested that airman would sometimes prefer to leave their station and walk a considerable distance to a pub, in order to obtain a pint of strong Burton Ale rather than drink the weak pints served in their local canteen. Hence, someone who had gone missing for a long time had 'Gone for a Burton'.

The facts and figures; names and specifications of the various weapons of war—whether they were aircraft, tanks or ships—were the currency of my youth. With a typical boy's love of lists, I had a 'Top Trumps'-like encyclopaedic knowledge of the fastest flying speeds of the aircraft; the calibres of the main gun of the tanks; and the normal displacement of the ships that found service during World War Two. And, all this information, would be used as a means of competition with my contemporaries, who would be similarly burdened by their own peculiar and specialised knowledge.

Looking back, it was strange what a cultural hold the Second World War still held over the 1970s. My mum and dad had both been children living in London during the War. They had experienced what it was like to be bombed, and they had witnessed the aftermath of bombing, but neither of them had been old enough to actually serve in any of the armed services. By the time that I was born, most of the physical infrastructure of my immediate neighbourhood, which had been damaged during the War had been repaired; rationing had long since stopped; the economy had returned to a more typical peace-time footing. It was the height of the Swinging Sixties, and London and England, as a whole, were making a concerted effort to make up for the deprivations of the previous two decades. Nevertheless, reminders of the Second World War were still everywhere. War movies were the most frequently-shown blockbusters of the day; classic novels, such as *Catch-22* by Joseph Heller, *Slaughterhouse Five* by Kurt Vonnegut, and *Gravity's Rainbow* by Thomas Pynchon returned to the War for their inspiration; and for kids, soldiers were the most popular toys.

However, one aspect of war, which was seldom mentioned was PTSD. The term 'shell-shock' was largely only talked about in relation to the First World War and the actual term PTSD (Post-Traumatic Stress Disorder) did not appear until 1980. In *Biggles in the Orient*, Johns does acknowledge the symptoms of a condition, which would now be called PTSD, in his description of some of the airmen working on airbases in India: "He knew only too well the symptoms resulting from nerve strain, shock and impotent anger." (p. 71). It might even represent a credit mark against Johns' name in the *Christie-Malry's-Own-Double-Entry*-style balance sheet that Mildred is keeping about him. Another credit might also be earned by the following statement that Biggles makes: "For the benefit of those of you who haven't been to India before, we don't use the expression *natives*. It's discourteous." (p. 34). Unfortunately, the expression that he advises instead is "coloured men" (p. 34), which might have Mildred reaching for her red pen to make a mark in the debit column. And is Mildred going to take up her cudgel in defence of the Japanese on top of all the other battles she is fighting? I don't think that there can be any distinctions or exemptions made. In for one, in for them all. That is the problem with trying to balance the books: you go hunting the one big debit only to discover that it is made up of lots of littler debits.

One enduring national stereotype that Johns relates regarding the Japanese, is that theirs is a 'copying culture'. Biggles comments: "The Japanese don't invent things—at least, not mechanical devices. They're good at copying other people's. They'll copy anything—they even copied their language from China." (p. 115). You say *poh-tay-toe*, I say *poh-tah-toe*. Perhaps there is a need for an additional line to be added to the glossary that Johns provides at the beginning of *Biggles in the Orient*: you say 'copying', I say 'importing'.

And 'Orient'? That's another whole can of worms.

My Best Friend the Pilot

While I was still entertaining fanciful notions of being a tramp when I left school (see *Don't Take Careers Advice from Novels (or Computers)*), one of my contemporaries was attempting to realise an ambition that he had held ever since he had been my best friend at junior school: to become a fighter pilot.

It was a very remarkable ambition for one so young. And it only really manifested itself in a single-minded determination to make flying his career. Whilst others of us were making model aircraft or, of course, reading our way through the stories of W. E. Johns, I don't recall that Gary was either an enthusiastic model-maker or an avid reader. For him, it was all about the real experience, not the secondary, vicarious substitute. And did he realise his ambition? I'm pleased to report: Yes, he did. He became an RAF fast-jet navigator and a qualified civil pilot, and it has been his vocation and his career until the inconvenient encroachment of years forced him into a less active and more advisory role.

On the other side of the planet, another friend of mine was also dreaming of being a pilot. His realisation of his ambitions came about not through the recognised career steps of an established path like the RAF, but by the equally hard graft of funding himself through flight-school, while he earned a living in an entirely different profession. Brendan started out as a Philips engineer in Australia, whilst attempting to gain sufficient experience and flying-hours to qualify to be a commercial pilot. I was fortunate enough to be a passenger with Brendan in a tiny two-seater, soon after he had gained his Private Pilot Licence.

We took off from Archerfield Airfield in the southern suburbs of Brisbane, and proceeded in a south-easterly direction towards the Gold Coast. I had donned a pair of headphones and strapped myself in to make myself look the part, but I never felt so much a piece of excess baggage as I did in that passenger seat, next to the pilot. The complex panel of instruments was a maze of technology beyond my comprehension. The various knobs, buttons and levers all a mystery in terms of their function. For all my Biggles reading, I realised that I didn't have the first idea of how to actually fly a plane in practice; only the scantest notion of how one even stayed aloft in terms of pure, scientific understanding. In an attempt to mask my pitiful ignorance, I asked Brandan what he used to navigate his course. In answer, he pointed out of the window, gesturing earthwards:

"You see that road down there. I just follow that."

It wasn't the sophisticated, technical reply, that I had been expecting.

All told, the journey to the coast was a run of about sixty miles, or so. It was not long before the inland waterways and familiar tall skyscrapers of Surfer's Paradise came into sight. We did a couple of circuits so that I could take photographs and then Brendan set the nose of the aircraft homeward-bound, following the precise same route back. Much as I thoroughly enjoyed the experience, I was relieved when we landed safe and sound a short time later.

If I didn't know it before, that short flight made me realise that, rather than my own dilettante approach to what I should do for a career—shall I be this; shall I be that?—to be a pilot was a genuine vocation, requiring years of dedication, hard work, responsibility, and expertise. It might suit Gary and Brendan and Biggles, but I knew that it was not for me. I think that vicarious pleasures are seriously underrated, and I am only too happy to limit my flying experience to the pages of W. E. Johns.

The *Golden Hind* and Glue Sniffing

As a child growing up in the Seventies, there was a lot to be scared of. I was scared of the Yorkshire Ripper. I was scared of punks. And I was scared of glue sniffers. Everywhere you turned there seemed to be the spectacle of adolescent youth, face buried into a crumpled paper bag, breathing in the toxic fumes of a cheap, over-the-counter solvent. Long before Spice arrived with the power to render its users catatonic on street corners and town centres, glue sniffers were a common sight in public parks and in remote corners of school playgrounds, long tendrils of Evo Stik dangling from their nostrils like an unfeasibly long bogey. While there seemed little danger of me becoming either a Yorkshire Ripper or a punk, the possibility of turning into a glue sniffer was an ever-present spectre, whilst I pursued such a potentially hazardous hobby: model making.

The two big manufacturers of model making kits were Airfix and Revell, and the range of vehicles that they produced was a plastic moulded sweetshop for a small boy. There were scale model replicas of tanks and armoured personnel carriers; jeeps and landing craft; mobile assault guns and officer's staff cars; and, of course, there were aircraft. It would have been possible to assemble an entire scale-model squadron of all the planes mentioned in *Biggles in the Orient*—both British and Japanese—from the kits available. For a novice model-maker, the choice was overwhelming; for a novice model-maker, some of the kits were also quite daunting. Some of the kits came with a huge number of separate pieces to assemble; the instructions were not always easy to comprehend; the decals and transfers fiddly to apply. With all these factors in mind, I can only presume that my dad was acting on the principle of 'sink or swim' when he bought for me as my very first model kit to assemble a 1/72 replica of Sir Francis Drake's Elizabethan flagship *Golden Hind.* It seemed to be made up of literally hundreds of pieces to assemble, each smaller than the last and, on top of that, it had moulded sails and endless rigging, which never failed to fall in anything but a complicated spider's web of knots and tangles. And then, to cap it all, the entire construction needed to be painted. I can still recall the difficulty of trying to paint the dozens of tiny replica cannons that lined the gun deck, whilst trying to avoid getting your fingers coated in shiny black enamel. Each Airfix or Revell kit listed the various paints that were required to create an authentic finish to your model. They came in individual miniature paint-pots made by Humbrol, distinguishable one from another either by a boring reference number or by a racy descriptive name: 'Battleship Grey'; 'Khaki Drill'; 'Gun Metal'.

And then there was the glue, or polystyrene adhesive, as it was then called. Each kit contained an inoffensive-looking, small tube of the stuff. Sufficient glue only to complete the particular model kit that accompanied it; only enough glue such that the tube often needed to be rolled up tight from the bottom end to provoke the last few precious drops to be squeezed out through the metal nozzle. Barely enough glue to moisten the very bottom of an ardent glue-sniffer's crumpled paper bag.

Yorkshire Ripper, punk, glue-sniffer? Ultimately, they were none of them for me. I remained too avid a model-maker to waste a single dab of polystyrene cement adhesive on any other activity.

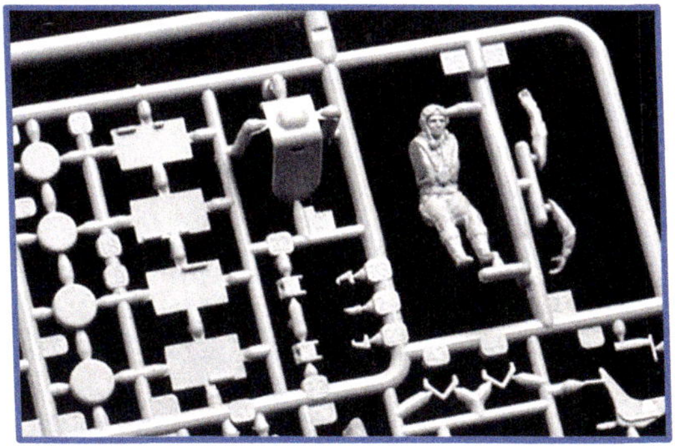

Everything Stops for Tea

Throughout the entire oeuvre of Biggles books from *The Camels are Coming*, published in 1932 to *Biggles Does Some Homework*, published in 1998, if there is one constant, it is that whatever Biggles is doing, he always finds time to eat a decent square meal. In *Biggles in the Orient*, he twice stops Air Commodore Raymond dead in his tracks in order to prioritise food ahead of duty: "'Just a minute, sir' protested Biggles, "I haven't had anything to eat today yet.—Give me a few minutes for a bath and a bite and I'll tell you all about it."' (p. 70).

In one of the later books in the series, *Biggles Sees Too Much* (Brockhampton, 1970), Biggles moves from "a dish of chips" (p. 98) to "bacon and egg" (p.59); a "Cornish tea" (p. 45) to "cold roast beef and boiled potatoes" (p. 98); "two packets of sandwiches" (p. 123) to "lobster" (p. 33) at the local pub. And when asked the question: "'What do you want now?"' (p. 122), he had only one definitive reply: "'Some food, what else?"' (p. 122).

In *Biggles Takes a Hand* (Brockhampton, 1963), Biggles even manages to contrive a stakeout of his main suspects in a restaurant. The restaurant that W. E. Johns describes is called the Adlon, located in Bank Street, Kensington, and run by Germans, the outside appearance being "…small, and while not exactly shabby it did not give the impression of being prosperous." (p. 9). Inside, however, Biggles discovers that the establishment was "not as cheap as he had expected" (p. 9) and "he counted fourteen tables, laid for parties of from two to four, fairly well spaced along a room that was long and rather narrow." (p. 9). While the name 'Adlon' is clearly taken from the famous Berlin hotel of the same name, I suggest that W. E. Johns' inspiration for the Adlon Restaurant might have been the legendary Daquise Restaurant in Thurloe Street, South Kensington. The Daquise is London's oldest Polish restaurant, first established in 1947, and has been a focal point for London's Polish community since the end of the Second World War. During the 1960s, when Johns was writing *Biggles Takes a Hand,* the restaurant witnessed meetings between Christine Keeler and Yevgeni Ivanov at the height of the Profumo Affair, and entertained Roman Polanski, fresh from filming *Repulsion* with Catherine Deneuve. During my own visit to

Daquise, I encountered neither political scandals or the Eastern European assassins that Biggles ran up against, but I can thoroughly recommend the meat dumplings.

When I was a child, 'tea' was an established mealtime, not just a hot beverage. Our recognised tea consisted of bread and dripping, the dripping being the congealed fat left over from the Sunday roast, spread across the bread as a substitute for butter. As a bonus, we would sometimes have cubes of the 'jelly' from the fat added on top in place of jam. This 'jelly' was the residue of the juices from the meat joint, once they had been cooled. It was a rare sight to find our fridge without a Pyrex bowl filled with congealed white dripping sitting atop a layer of glistening orange jelly. Nowadays, I shudder at the memory; at the time, I used to lap up the stuff as though it were manna from heaven. This description of such a childhood tea might suggest that we were a somewhat impoverished household. Far from it. By the time that I was a twinkle in my parents' eye, our family had already made the difficult transition from 'London poor' to 'suburban comfortable'; had transcended from 'working class' to 'middle class' in every recognisable extent. The beef dripping tea was a throwback. It had its roots in a different time; in a time of war; and a time of hardship, which was not so easily shed, or forgotten.

Reading #10: *Biggles in the Baltic*

"...and that consequently this country is at war with Germany." W. E. Johns records it slightly differently at the start of *Biggles in the Baltic* (Oxford, 1940): "England is now, therefore, in a state of war with Germany." (p. 9), but it is a mere quibble over semantics given the backdrop of such a devastating world event. What is more surprising is Biggles' reaction to the monumental announcement: "'Well, that's that.'" (p. 9). I don't think that I would ever have such *sang-froid* in similar circumstances.

I have been fortunate enough to live through a period of relative peace in terms of day-to-day living; only the IRA have ever brought a degree of violence to London such that it consciously impinged on my cossetted existence. Most of the recent wars that have involved British servicemen have been fought in distant lands—the Falkland Islands; Afghanistan; Iraq, amongst others. Neville Chamberlain's shattering announcement on 3 September 1939 signalled the start of a conflict, which would bring the horrors of war to the very shores of these islands, and affect the lives of a civilian population in a way previously unexperienced.

As a previous combatant, Biggles is called up on the very day that war is announced and, within a week, is given a special mission, which takes him to a small island in the middle of the Baltic Sea, close to the coast of Germany. During what is a relatively short-lived tenure on this remote outpost of war, either Biggles, or one of his companions, manages to go missing—

sometimes supposed dead—at fairly frequent intervals, and this provides W. E. Johns an opportunity to indulge one of his most well-used, but also most effective, forms of story construction: the "What Happened to…" chapter heading. In *Biggles in the Baltic*, we get "What Happened to Algy" (pp 111-123) and "What Happened to Biggles" (pp 136-149). The first ever appearance of the "What Happened to…" chapter heading occurs in *The Black Peril,* with another "What Happened to Algy"; we get our first "What Happened to Ginger" in *Biggles Hits the Trail*; another "Algy" in *Biggles & Co.*; a glut of "What Happened"s in *Biggles Flies West* with "What Happened to Dick" and the first appearance of a "What Happened to Biggles"; and "Algy" featuring again in *Biggles Flies South* (Oxford, 1938) before "Ginger" gets another look in, in *Biggles in the South Seas.* And what can we deduce from all this? That Algy is perhaps the most accident-prone of the adventurous trio, and the most likely to end up in a situation from which he needs to be rescued? Or, perhaps that he is the most expendable, allowing either Biggles or Ginger to be cast in the more heroic role of rescuer. Even Algy eventually finds himself slightly put out at this particular status quo, commenting towards the end of *Biggles in the Baltic*: "'You might give me credit for something once in a while.'" (p. 252). It is a clever plot device, though, for building up a sense of suspense, and not dissimilar to that used by Dan Brown in *The Da Vinci Code*: leaving one of the protagonists in a situation of mortal danger; keeping the reader hanging in anticipation of the outcome, while progressing the stories of other characters; only to return to resolve the original situation several chapters later.

Biggles in the Baltic also contains an interesting allusion to the 'butterfly effect'. While Biggles rarely allows himself the indulgence of philosophising within the realm of conditionals—as Johns writes: "It is often fascinating, if futile, to speculate what might have happened if certain events had gone otherwise than they did." (p. 125)—Ginger finds himself in that classic situation of Robert Frost's *The Road Not Taken*: "Two roads diverged in the woods, and I… I took the one less travelled by, and that has made all the difference." With the consequence that "the history of 'Z' Squadron would have been altogether different from what it actually was." (p. 125).

My Dad's War

My dad was ten years old when the Second World War started, and sixteen years old when it ended. Not for him the experience of many of his contemporaries as an evacuee to the countryside. He spent the entire duration of the war living in a suburb of north London, which was regularly bombed during the Blitz from September 1940 to May 1941, and was then intermittently bombed from June 1944 to March 1945 when Germany developed the V-1 flying bombs and V-2 rockets. Of all the various bombs that landed in his neighbourhood, my dad described the V-1 'Doodlebug' as being the most frightening.

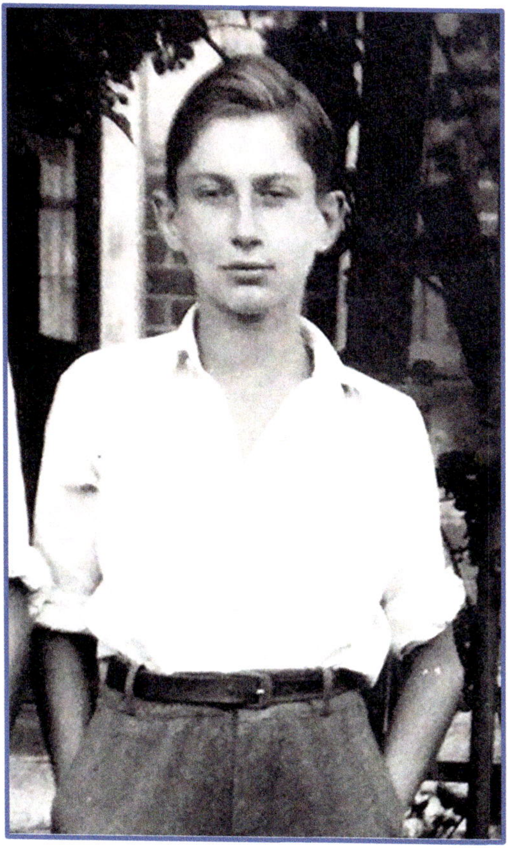

The V-1—officially *Vergeltungswaffe* 1, or Vengeance Weapon 1—announced itself in the sky with a distinctive buzzing sound, like an angry hornet or a poorly tuned motorbike. But it was not the *sound* of the V-1 that anyone on the ground feared; it was the silence. The moment that that distinctive sound stopped was the moment to be worried. At the point that the V-1's engine cut out, it began to fall to earth, delivering an explosive charge of almost two thousand pounds of Amatol-39, a mixture of TNT and ammonium nitrate. In contrast, the V-2s were silent, and struck without warning.

At the time, the family home was relatively close to Northolt Aerodrome, which was a recognisable target for German bombing raids. RAF Northolt was home to a number of Polish fighter squadrons flying Hawker Hurricanes during the Battle of Britain and, later, Supermarine Spitfires and de Havilland Mosquitos. Luftwaffe raids on the airfield meant that some of the earliest bombs to fall on London actually fell on Harrow during the early hours of 22 August 1940.

My dad's family had an Anderson shelter constructed at the end of their garden. Other homes in the area had a Morrison shelter inside their houses. The Anderson shelter was constructed of six curved sheets of corrugated steel, joined together and then half buried, with earth piled on top. In appearance, they look not dissimilar to the conventional idea of a 'Hobbit-hole', a design that has received a modern resurgence in interest being frequently used for *chi-chi* glamping pods. Each shelter was designed to house four adults and two children. The Morrison shelter was more like a metal cage, with a solid steel-plate table-top roof, and a mattress floor. Although my dad made some use of the Anderson shelter at the start of the War whenever the air raid warning sirens sounded, the refuge quickly became cold and uncomfortable and water-logged and, common with many families, was rapidly abandoned; a warm bed being preferred, and a *laissez faire* attitude of 'what will be, will be' being adopted regarding the bombing.

Similar to the mischievous activities of the Outlaws so vividly described in Richmal Crompton's 'William' books, my dad and his friends would search the bomb craters and blown-up buildings of their neighbourhood for pieces of shrapnel left over from the fallen bombs; a considerable competition ensuing to find the largest and most intact pieces. However, my dad was neither possessed with the mind of an archivist nor troubled with a bump for nostalgia and, whereas I would have hung on to any of these trophies long into adulthood, nothing that resulted from his wartime scavenging still survives. With his friends, he would play at being soldiers and spies, and he would attempt to recognise the various different aircraft that crisscrossed the skies above his house, both friend and foe; often being able to distinguish the individual planes from their engine sound alone: the throaty purr of the British Rolls-Royce Merlin engines; the more nasal whine of the German DB (Daimler-Benz) engines; the deep bass drones of the big bombers as compared to the rhythmic whistle of the smaller fighters. It might have been a skill learned from Biggles: "'They're our boys, too, if I know the sweet song of Merlin engines.'" (*Biggles Defies the Swastika*, p. 173).

And, amidst all the extraordinariness of the times—of the news from the frontline, the sometime threat of invasion, the ambiguousness of what the future would bring, and the ever-present danger of being bombed—normal life carried on. There was still school to go to; best friends to be made and lost; lessons to be learned; exams to be sat; football matches to be played. The daily routine of life still played out on an individual level, even while the larger backdrop of history remained so uncertain. And, taking everything into consideration, my dad would probably say that he had a 'good war'. He didn't lose anyone immediately close to him; the family home withstood the Luftwaffe's best attempts to raise it to the ground; he survived, where so many others were not so fortunate and, in that survival, he was shaped in a way, which no other kind of education could have fashioned.

Would my dad have wished his childhood to be any different? As I have mentioned, he was no sentimentalist; I think that he would have been someone to echo Biggles' words at the start of *Biggles in the Baltic*: "Well, that's that." (p. 9).

Back Garden Morse

Consistent with the fickle nature of childhood best friends, by the time that I reached secondary school, my best friend was no longer would-be pilot Gary (see *My Best Friend the Pilot*), but had been replaced by accomplished junior violin and piano player Andrew.

Andrew lived in a street that ran perpendicular to my own one and, as the crow flies, our houses were separated by a distance of about 150 metres. Although we didn't attend the same secondary school, we used to see each other practically every day after school and most of the time during the weekends. As if this were not saturation enough, we developed a scheme whereby we could communicate with one another even when we were each safely ensconced in our own separate houses. In an age pre-mobile phone, the walkie-talkie was the state-of-the-art piece of kit when it came to mobile, person-to-person communications, but such technology was way beyond the means of the average schoolboy, even one flush from the profits of his leaflet delivery round (see *A Nice Little Earner*). The recognised home-made alternative was two plastic cups, or two metal cans, joined together by a taut piece of string. Andrew and I experimented with this set-up for some time, attempting to perfect a workable design; eventually giving up when we realised that it allowed audible communication over no greater distance than it was possible to simply shout. What would Biggles do? This probably wasn't a conscious thought on my part, but something of Biggles' innovativeness must have imparted itself to me through my boyhood of reading. There must be a solution to our communications problem. The solution lay amidst the pages of *Biggles in the Baltic*: Morse code.

Based on the remote, rocky island of Bergen Ait, Biggles uses Morse code to communicate secret messages back to his headquarters in Britain. The job of relaying the messages falls to young Roy Smyth, one of the newest recruits to Biggles' team. Roy is in charge of the precious codebook, which Biggles ensures is always kept under lock and key, to prevent it falling into the hands of the enemy: "He unlocked a small safe and took out a red book carrying on the front in large letters, the word SECRET." (p. 32). Following Biggles' example, Andrew and I set about learning the

Morse alphabet. My previous knowledge only ran to the classic signal for SOS and, even then, I was fairly hazy as to whether it was three dots followed by three dashes followed by three dots, or three dashes followed by three dots followed by three dashes. However, we were conscientious in our task, and it was not long before we had memorised the entire code; we even added a couple of additional signals of our own, which we thought might be useful: five dots for "repeat" and five dashes for "I'm going now".

From the window of Andrew's bedroom, he could look out directly across a dozen or so gardens to my house and garden. I had the same view from my bedroom window, but it was at an oblique angle, meaning that I had to either lean out of the window or squint sideways as best I could. Our plan was to use electric torches to signal to each other across the intervening gardens, using Morse code for our messages. An unanticipated problem arose almost straight away. It was summer time and it did not get sufficiently dark to signal until past ten o'clock, by which time we were both supposed to be tucked up in our respective beds and fast asleep. The plan was shelved until the autumn.

Long summer days passed, the new school term began and, little by little, the nights began to draw in to find Andrew and I, noses pressed to our bedroom windows, torches in hand, Morse code books in front of us. It was a thrilling moment to see the first flash of electric light beam out from Andrew's window, penetrating the obscurity of the dark gardens. But was it a dot or a dash? What was the message? I quickly flashed back five dots to "repeat". Andrew was clearly having similar problems understanding my messages; his reply to my "repeat" was five dots to "repeat" as well. After several failed attempts, I sent out the signal of five dashes, signifying that "I'm going now." The last signal I saw from Andrew's window was another five dots: "repeat". All things considered, calling on the landline was probably just easier.

The Naming of Parts

Lists play an important part in almost all boys' lives. Solar System; How Life Began; The World We Live In; Population; The Wonders of Nature; Codes; The Weather; Time; Communications; Travel; Space; Sport; Medicine; Invention and Discovery; Science and Mathematics; Money; Prime Ministers and Presidents; Kings and Queens; Orders of Chivalry; British Flags; The Law; Religion; British Hallmarks on Gold and Silver Wares; The Arts: it is a list of the contents of one of my most frequently referred to books, when I was a child: *The Piccolo Encyclopedia of Useful Facts* edited by Jean Stroud. For all its long contents, it was actually quite a small, compact book; a small, yellow paperback, which contained within its 216 pages, all the possible information that a knowledge-hungry adolescent could want to know about the world, that is excepting the chapter on British Hallmarks on Gold and Silver Wares, which even I considered a field of information too far.

In *Biggles in the Baltic*, it is with this same spirit of boyish enthusiasm for lists and classification that Ginger sets about naming the airplanes of their squadron. Having established a theme of Australian titles, it is not long before he has christened his only plane *Dingo*; Algy's plane *Didgeree-du*; Biggles' plane *Willie-Willie*; and "'What about the spare machine? The duck-billed platypus is the only other Australian animal I know.'" (*Biggles in the Baltic*, p. 25). Personally, for the sake of consistency, and having started with two names both beginning with the letter 'D', I would have been more tempted to christen the last two planes *Dinkum* and *Digger*, but that's just me being a bit anal. A bit *more* anal.

Having always been a lover of nature, some of my earliest encounters with classification centred around animals and dinosaurs. Without being entirely cognisant of the individual distinctions, I instinctively warmed to the Linnaean System of Classification—Kingdom; Phylum; Class; Order; Family; Genus; Species—for its inherent tidiness. It was rather like ordering the clothes in my chest of drawers into jumpers and pants and socks, and then within that, into small jumpers and small pants and small socks, and then within that into small red jumpers and small red pants and small red socks. It kept together things that were similar, and made instantly recognisable things that were different. Classification taps into a basic human fear of the unknown. It brings order and security. But might it also be guilty of widening gulfs between opposites? And missing opportunities to discover something entirely knew?

Working amongst the ivory towers of a university environment for the past thirty years, I have often been surprised by the tapering nature of research: the greater the knowledge, seemingly the more focussed and narrow that knowledge becomes, often to the exclusion of entire other fields of learning. In Britain, this approach to education begins at a relatively young age; by the time most students have reached the age of sixteen they have already cast off most of the subjects in the curriculum in favour of just three specialised 'A' Levels; at university, the trend towards specialisation becomes even more pronounced. Interdisciplinary learning is not greatly practised, unlike in somewhere like France, where the *baccalauréat* permits a wider range of subjects to be studied for longer, including multiple foreign languages, philosophy and even physical education.

Culturally, as well as educationally, I fear that we are heading towards a more divided world, largely because of our collective persistence in adopting a silo mentality towards cross-party thinking: in politics; in education; in work; and in trying to consider such important topics as climate change, and identity, and gender, and race. While W. E. Johns may have got a lot wrong in terms of his less than politically correct language and recidivist colonial attitude, in the context of his times, he was someone who recognised the importance of diversity; was endlessly fascinated by the complex and varied scope of our world and all the people that inhabit it; managed to capture in his writing the excitement of all of Earth's endless possibilities for at least one, wide-eyed, curious child. While it would be unfair of me to accuse Mildred of possessing a silo mentality without getting to know her a bit better, nevertheless, at this—roughly—halfway point of my investigations, I am of the opinion that, it is better to embrace the world and learn from all its failings, rather than attempt to obliterate them.

Nowadays, I still like lists and classification and order, but I'm also not adverse to wearing one red sock and one blue sock sometimes.

Reading #11: *Biggles Defies the Swastika*

The first three books, which W. E. Johns wrote about Biggles in the Second World War, all centre around the conflict taking place in Scandinavia and the Baltic states—*Biggles in the Baltic* (Oxford, 1940); *Biggles Sees It Through* (Oxford, 1941); and *Biggles Defies the Swastika* (Oxford, 1941). It might seem like an unusual theatre of war to focus upon, and even Biggles complains that he would rather be in France: "Biggles had listened without enthusiasm, for he was quite content to be where he was." (p. 10). It must be remembered, though, that during the first eight months after Chamberlain's declaration of a state of war between Britain and Germany, there was comparatively little fighting between the two nations; it was the period of the 'Phoney War'. The event, which ended this status quo, was Germany's invasion of Denmark and Norway on 9 April 1940, Operation Weserübung. This represented Germany's first major offensive on the Western Front, and was swiftly followed, a month later, by the invasions of Holland, Belgium and Luxemburg and then, ultimately, France.

It must have been a difficult time for Johns to be writing. The character of Biggles had always been that of someone who had won through despite the odds, but there had also always been an authenticity to the stories, and an importance set in adhering to the facts and, in 1940, the facts were that Britain was not doing very well in the War. Johns must have found himself torn between a chronicler's instinct to record the existing facts and a patriotic duty to produce a story, which would boost public morale. In France, Britain was facing a heroic, but ultimately humiliating, retreat from Dunkirk, whereas in Norway, Johns could at least relate a victory, albeit only a temporary one, in the battle for Narvik, until the advent of Operation Alphabet, which resulted in the total evacuation of Allied troops from Norway between 24 May and 8 June 1940.

In the early Biggles books set during the Second World War, it feels almost as if Biggles is fighting a lone crusade against a greater, mighty power, perhaps mirroring Britain's sense of isolation? It is not until *Spitfire Parade* (Oxford, 1941), with its backdrop of the Battle of Britain, that there is a sense of Biggles joining up with a wider squadron of combatants, and fighting a war more universal in its scope and influence.

Johns choice of title is interesting, too: *Biggles Defies the Swastika.* Not *Biggles Defies the Nazis.* Or *Biggles Defies Germany.* But *Biggles Defies the Swastika.* The swastika had become emblematic with the Nazi Party in Germany as early as 1920, where it was displayed facing clockwise, rotated 45 degrees, on a white circle against a red background. Nowadays, it is hard to think of the symbol in any other context, but its origins are far, far older, and its original meaning entirely different.

The swastika is an ancient religious symbol, the word first appearing in South Asia around 500BCE. The origin of the word is from the Sanskrit term *svastika*, meaning 'well-being'. It remains a symbol of spirituality for many Indian religions. In the western world, the symbol was originally recognised as a sign of peace and good fortune, even appearing in Coca-Cola advertising campaigns. It first became linked to antisemitism in Romania prior to the First World War, and its association with white supremacism has persisted although, in the 21st century, there has been a campaign to reclaim the swastika for its original, religious meaning, and to call the symbol as used by the Nazis the *hakenkreuz*, in order to make a clear distinction.

Johns makes frequent reference to the swastika, particularly in the early pages of *Biggles Defies the Swastika*, where the symbol represents the invading force; its sudden proliferating across Norway emblematic of the speed and decisiveness of the Nazi advance. It is interesting to note, though, that in *Biggles Sees It Through*, published in the same month as *Biggles Defies the Swastika*, the symbol of the swastika is displayed on two planes flown by Biggles himself, as can be seen in Howard Leigh's illustration of a Bristol Blenheim on the front cover of that book and a Gloucester Gladiator on the frontispiece. The reason for this apparent anomaly is that in *Biggles Sees It Through*, Biggles and his companions find themselves flying for an international squadron supporting the Finns in their war with Russia and, since its inception in 1918, the symbol of the Finnish Air Force had been the swastika. In contrast, the Luftwaffe, although adopting the image of an eagle holding a swastika for its emblem, actually displayed on the fuselage of its aircraft the *Balkenkreuz*, a straight-armed cross, which can be seen displayed on four Messerschmitt Bf 109s also on the front cover of *Biggles Sees It Through.*

Whereas in *Biggles Sees It Through*, Biggles is accompanied by Algy, Ginger and Smyth, in *Biggles Defies the Swastika* we find Biggles as a solitary point of resistance, even betrayed by some of his former Norwegian colleagues, a duplicity that Biggles considers even worse than that of the invaders: "Three of the members of the flying club were in German pay… what he could not understand, and what he could not forgive, was a man playing traitor to his own country… men who were far worse than spies; they were renegades, traitors in the most despicable sense." (p. 26).

Of course, this treachery by a small minority of Norwegians brought a new word into the English language: Quisling. Vidkun Quisling was a politician and Nazi collaborator who nominally led the Norwegian government during its occupation by Germany. The term 'Quisling' has since entered common English language to refer to a turncoat or a collaborator. *The Times*, in 1940, commented about the word that: "Aurally it contrives to suggest something at once slippery and tortuous." By, 1941, even William Brown in *William Does His Bit* (Newnes, 1941) has heard of Quisling: "'I say,' he said, 'who is this Grisling man?'... 'No, dear," said Mrs Brown patiently. 'This particular man was a Norwegian and helped the Germans to get a footing in his country, and other people in other countries who try to do the same, are all called Quisling.'" (*William Does His Bit*, p. 7).

Make Do and Mend

Although the concept of recycling might be seen as a relatively modern idea as a tool in the battle against global warming, there was a far more greatly entrenched recycling spirit amongst the generation who lived through the Second World War. Indeed, W. E. Johns, himself, was a great recycler. His book *Spitfire Parade* (Oxford, 1941) is proof of that.

Spitfire Parade is subtitled *Stories of Biggles in War-time.* But, which war? Ostensibly, *Spitfire Parade* is an anthology of short stories recounting Biggles exploits as commander of 666 (Fighter) Squadron, flying missions during the Battle of Britain against the Luftwaffe. It is also where we encounter hereafter series character Lord Bertie Lissie for the first time in a Biggles book, plus a number of other pilots in his squadron, who are destined to become Biggles irregulars. These include Angus Mackail, ex-pugilist Tug Carrington, accident prone Welshman Taffy Hughes, American Tex O'Hara, George 'Ferocity' Ferris and Henry Harcourt.

However, all is not quite as it might seem. Many of the short stories from *Spitfire Parade* are actually simply rewrites from stories that originally appeared in book form in either *The Camels are Coming* or in *Biggles in France* (Amalgamated Press, 1935) and, at that time, the stories were not about the Second World War but were about the First World War. Johns must have been under pressure to release some morale-boosting stories about Biggles'—and Britain's—success in the Battle of Britain and, rather than hurriedly write new material, he became an early advocate of a design for living that would later in 1943 become a Ministry of Information campaign: 'Make Do and Mend'.

It was perhaps an inevitable act of rebellion by the children of the 'Make Do and Mend' generation that they would create an economic system that relies on in-built obsolescence to generate growth. It may need the children of this subsequent generation to similarly rebel against the rampant consumerism of their parents in order to tackle the problems of climate change, which pose the greatest threat to their own peace.

Reading #12: *Biggles Sweeps the Desert*

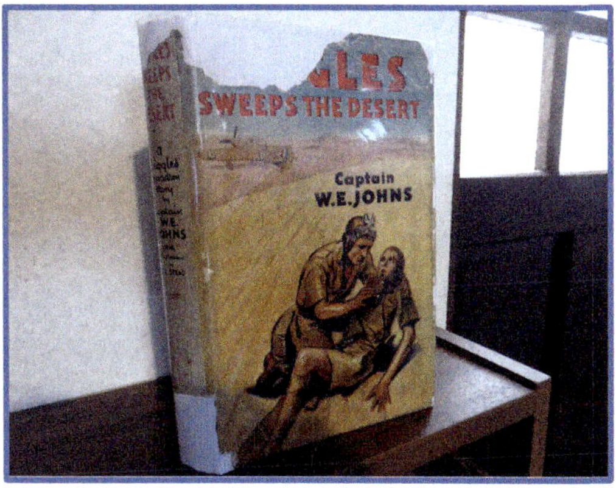

First, a bibliographical note: *Biggles Sweeps the Desert* is the first original Biggles book to be published by Hodder and Stoughton (following an earlier reissue of *Biggles Flies East*). It does not quite mark W. E. Johns' complete break from Oxford University Press, but the end is clearly nigh. It also represents a departure from the fantastic cover illustrations by Howard Leigh; quite pointedly, the dust jacket of *Biggles Sweeps the Desert* contains the wording: "With illustrations by L. L. Stead". I also find the dust jacket amusing for the fact that the blurb on the rear cover manages to give away the entire plot of the book in three concise paragraphs. No spoiler warnings in those days!

For anyone who failed to read the jacket blurb, I will reveal that in *Biggles Sweeps the Desert*, Biggles finds himself thrown into the unfamiliar position of encountering an enemy air ace possessing flying skills every bit as adept as his own. Where Erich von Stalhein often fulfils the role of Biggles' counterpart on the ground; in Hauptmann von Zoyton, Biggles finds an adversary who is able to match his abilities in the air. The plot of the book centres around the duel between these two rivals in their attempts to gain the upper hand over one another.

The western concept of a duel between two protagonists to settle a dispute evolved from the Viking *holmgang* and the medieval judicial law of trial by combat. The first code of duelling appeared in Renaissance Italy and, with it, the concept of a contest being settled between gentlemen, carrying with it something of the chivalric order of an earlier time. The Trial by Battle Abolition Bill of 1819 criminalised duelling in Britain, although the last recorded duel was not until several decades later in 1852. The French, who perhaps retain a closer attachment to an old code of chivalry introduced during the Carolingian Empire at the time of Charlemagne, were still fighting duels as late as 1967.

The popular image of a duel is one contested either by pistols or swords. In the case of Biggles and von Zoyton, their duel is fought between Supermarine Spitfire and Messerschmitt 109 F. However, the idea of a duel fought between two gentlemen is retained: Biggles gentlemanly credentials are, of course, never in doubt; and, in von Zoyton, it is shown by his actions that he is similarly made of the 'right stuff', even if his subsequent behaviour in *Sergeant Bigglesworth CID* (Hodder, 1947) lets him down. It is a brave decision of Johns to not show all Germans as pantomime villains, particularly at the time that the book was written; perhaps better reflecting the complicated patterns of enmity and friendship, suspicion and respect, which have long existed between the two nations over many centuries.

While the desert of southern Libya provides the battleground for the duel between Biggles and von Zoyton; a virtual blank canvas that the British and the Germans can seemingly carve up and divide as they choose, the original inhabitants of the region are not altogether overlooked in the book. Although the Tuareg—or 'Toureg' in Johns' description—are reduced to the role of merely subservient helpers of the Germans, aspects of their Arabic language are given greater recognition.

Italicised to highlight their foreign nature, the unfamiliar words were instantly seized upon and assimilated by my younger self: words like *haboob* and *gumbaz*. They were words outside of my dictionary; ones where I could only infer their meaning by their context in the story. *Haboob* was relatively easy, since there was an entire chapter devoted to the subject, as a huge sand storm swept up to engulf Biggles and his squadron. *Gumbaz* was not so obvious, although it was clearly a form of clothing: "…his *gumbaz* was being wrapped round his head, blinding him and suffocating him with its voluminous folds" (p. 106). The *gumbaz* is actually a long-sleeved coat, maybe more typical of the Bedouin or of Palestinian origin, rather than belonging to the Tuareg but, even if Johns was slightly cavalier in mixing-and-matching his various dialects of Arabic, I was grateful to him for exposing me to a vocabulary of words from other languages at an early age.

Looking at another aspect of language, *Biggles Sweeps the Desert* is a good example of the power of Johns' descriptive capabilities. He manages to evoke a keen sense of place, even when describing lands and events where it is unlikely that he ever had the opportunity to either visit, or witness, first-hand himself. In describing the *haboob*, which overtakes Biggles, he manages to cram in alliteration, metaphor, onomatopoeia; even if he does combine a few similes: "Dunes rose and fell like a storm-tossed ocean, the tops tumbling and smoking like miniature volcanos." (p. 125).

Don't ask me who's the bloke on the back, I don't know.

The Difficult Concept of Honour

Honour: what does it mean? Probably very different things to different people. For some people, it will have no meaning whatsoever; will be a concept outside of their ordinary ken. For others, it will be a defining principle, which dictates almost every aspect of their life. *Biggles Sweeps the Desert* is all about honour, and the different ways that it manifests itself resulting in particular codes of conduct and patterns of behaviour. For W. E. Johns, honour is clearly an important thing; also, that it is a *good* thing. This may seem like a given, but honour is such a complicated human construct that it has the potential to lead people into modes of behaviour, which by no measurable standard can be considered 'good', such as the so-called honour killings that take place in certain societies, and which are often linked to religion, caste, social status or sexuality. Johns makes his position abundantly clear by the simple fact that the British contingent of his story all behave in a way that is considered honourable and, by and large, are rewarded for it; and the Germans—von Zoyton excepted—behave in a way that is decidedly dishonourable, and are correspondingly punished.

The first way in which the British appear in a more honourable light than the Germans is in the fact that they have far fewer resources at their disposal than their enemy: "...we are outnumbered six to one." (p. 187). There has always been honour attached to a situation of fighting against the odds; kudos when a smaller force has been able to overcome a larger one. It is the classic story of David and Goliath; Rorke's Drift; Agincourt. In such circumstances, there is even honour in defeat, witness the Battle of Thermopylae. Honour is not meant to be something that can be easily won.

Biggles Sweeps the Desert sees another example of a German reneging once having given his parole, as was the case in *The Rescue Flight*, and with much the same result. Prisoner of war Leutnant Heinrich Hymann promises Biggles that he will not try to escape, for which he is given certain privileges: "'I don't think even a Nazi would break his parole.'" (p. 72). However, Biggles' faith is proved not to be justified: "'If Biggles has a weakness, it is judging other people by his own principles.'" (pp. 71-72). Hymann escapes, only to be shot down in a case of mistaken identity by one of his own airmen: "'Hymann's lying didn't get him far.'" (p. 93).

Another example of honour takes the form of an almost chivalric code existing between fighter pilots. When engaged in combat, Biggles sees it as a point of honour never to be the first to turn away if he finds himself meeting an enemy plane head-on: "He had no intention of turning away, for the first to turn away in head-on attack admits inferiority, and one of the first traditions laid down by the Flying Corps in the early days of air combat was 'never turn'." (p. 143).

Other examples of honourable behaviour recounted throughout the book are actions such as burying the dead of the enemy, a case of do as to others as you would have done to yourself; and not leaving enemy forces to be killed for no reason, making a clear distinction between killing in the course of duty during wartime and killing as cold-blooded murder: "'It's one thing to shoot a man in a scrap, but a horse of a different colour to drop him in the sand and leave him to the mercy of a *haboob*. Only a skunk would do a thing like that.'" (p. 123). And, of course, there is the simple honour of sticking by and supporting your friends; a principle, which we see Biggles stick to time and time again, often at the risk of endangering his own life.

In Britain, the concept of honour has often become entangled with the equally complicated system of class. Honour was considered the preserve of 'gentlemen' and the public school system. That Johns must have identified with this belief, too, is evident in the fact that he ascribes a knowledge of honour to the German air ace von Zoyton, who displays all the characteristic of a 'gentleman', whilst still remaining a Nazi.

As if to reinforce the background message of the book, the closing line in *Biggles Sweeps the Desert* is "'The honour's mine,' he said." (p. 208).

In my secondary school, a system of honour existed, regardless of the fact that it was not a public school. It was a feral, classroom honour; a primeval, instinctive knowledge that existed between boys, learned and adhered to despite any formal tuition. One of the most fundamental forms in which this playground honour took shape was in the unwritten understanding that you did not 'squeal' on any of your contemporaries. The greatest crime was to be a 'grass'. The most frequent consequence of this was for an entire class to be detained in detention because of the actions of one individual whom no one else would give away. Of course, a more sophisticated system of honour would have obliged the guilty pupil to own up to his crimes for the sake of his classmates, but such was often not the case.

Our first-year class already well established, one boy had the misfortune to join the group late on into the summer term. It was not easy for him to make friends amongst cliques that had already formed and alliances that had already gelled. It was perhaps inevitable that he fell a victim of bullying and isolation. In a hostile environment, I was one of the few people to befriend him. Now, it may sound like I am recounting this anecdote for my own self-aggrandisement, but that is not the case. In fact, quite the opposite. You see, I let my friend down. I didn't adhere to one of Biggles' basic principles of sticking by his friend. The reason why? It was all a complicated question of honour.

The problem was that my new friend broke the fundamental rule of the classroom; he acted against accepted playground honour: he squealed on his bullies. It was a perfectly understandable thing to do; it was a perfectly logical thing to do; but, at the same time, it was just not done. I was thrown into a quandary. Should I stick by my friend, or should I join with the herd and condemn his action? Peter in the high priest's courtyard, I chose the latter course. Is that a rooster I hear crowing around the playground? It is a decision, which still troubles me to this day. What would have been the honourable thing to do?

Modern-day whistleblowers still face this same kind of dilemma. Even when the end justifies the means, there still remains a certain amount of prejudice against the whistleblowers themselves.

Honour: it's a funny old thing. I am still trying to work it out.

An Intense Concentration of Self

If I temporarily leave the works of W. E. Johns to one side, one of my favourite books is *Moby Dick* by Herman Melville. Everyone knows the story of *Moby Dick*—big whale; mad captain, hell bent on revenge; intermittent Biblical allusions—however, for me, one of the most compelling passages within the book involves one of the more minor characters: Pip, the cabin boy.

In Chapter 93: *The Castaway*, Pip joins Stubb's boat on a whale-hunt, only to find himself, in the confusion of the hunt, cast overboard; left floating in the ocean as the boat quickly recedes beyond the horizon: "…the awful lonesomeness is intolerable. The intense concentration of self in the middle of such a heartless immensity."

It is a powerful image, alone and adrift in the ocean, thrown back on your own resources to the exclusion of all others; a terrifying experience, which ultimately sends Pip insane.

Perhaps because of his youthfulness, it is often Ginger who is cast in the 'Pip' role in the Biggles books. I do not know if loneliness weighs more heavily on youth than it does for adults but, in Ginger, W. E. Johns finds a surprisingly contemplative mouthpiece to describe the nature of the emotion. Johns does an effective job at mixing up the circumstances of Ginger's abandonments, too.

In *Biggles Sweeps the Desert*, it is perhaps inevitable that Ginger will become lost in the desert, alone without water, isolated from the rest of his squadron: "There was not a sign of life—not an insect, not a blade of grass." (p. 36) only "…an unimaginable silence, a silence so profound that every sound he made was magnified a hundredfold." (p. 36). In this kind of environment, Ginger is quick to realise that "In such a place, a man would soon lose his reason." It was not long before "The loneliness and the silence became unbearable, and he began to shout for the sake of hearing a human voice." (p. 43). In the same way that Pip quickly descended into madness in *Moby Dick*, Ginger finds it hard to hold onto his sanity. Even when flying over such an empty wilderness, Ginger is "…not immune from the feeling of depression it creates.

Assailed by a sense of loneliness, as though he alone was left in a world that had died." (p. 20).

It is another arena of isolation that Johns returns to quite frequently: the loneliness of flying and the crushing weight of responsibility of being in sole charge of an aircraft, separated from any external aid or support. (see *Reading 2: The Rescue Flight*). But there is also another form of loneliness to be discovered in the air; that experienced while parachuting. In *Biggles Sweeps the Desert*, Ginger describes his feelings during a jump: "He appeared to be suspended in space. In fact, he was not conscious of any sensation at all, except perhaps one of loneliness. He appeared to be alone in the world." (p. 157).

In *Biggles Defies the Swastika*, Ginger finds himself having to ditch his aircraft into the sea, resulting in a situation more physically akin to that experienced by poor Pip: "There was absolutely nothing he could do except climb on to the centre-section and stare dumbly into the leaden darkness that surrounded him. Except for a gentle slap of wavelets against the hull of his machine, silence reigned." (*Biggles Defies the Swastika*, p. 210). More terrifying, still, is his experience in *Biggles in the South Seas*, where he becomes trapped in an underwater cavern: "The darkness was intense. The only sound was the eerie gurgling of the rising and falling water." (*Biggles in the South Seas*, p. 155). Once again, Ginger's mental resolve is tested: "He became a victim of every sort of pessimism. He fancied that the swirl of water increased, as if a struggle was going on in the cave. He imagined that he could see dark shadows moving just inside the entrance." (*Biggles in the South Seas*, p. 158).

Of course, Ginger's earliest abandonment was that by his parents. When Biggles first discovers him, he is alone, having run away from home and a father, whom one imagines had little spare time to show him affection, and a mother who is not mentioned: "My father's a miner; he fetched me a clip of the ear when I told him I was going to be a pilot, so I hopped it." (*The Black Peril*, p. 44). Is it too far-fetched to suggest that Johns' constant positioning of Ginger in positions of friendless peril is all an analogy for this first rejection? Or is that taking Biggles into psychological realms too deep? Perhaps. After all, there is only so far you can take an analogy, even when it is a good one.

As I have mentioned before, I am an only child. An only child, but not a lonely child. I think that I can truly say that I don't know what the experience of loneliness feels like. But then how would I know? It is not something like sex where, if I had been getting it wrong all these years, I would presume that someone would have told me by now; loneliness, by its nature, is a very personal emotion, not easily quantified.

My younger self would frequently build dens beneath the dining room table; pulling down the tablecloth so that it shut out the outside world; stocking it with toys and provisions such that I could hole-up for hours at a time and escape into a private world entirely of my own. I find it interesting that both Pip and Ginger feel the pressure of what Melville so evocatively describes as "The intense concentration of self." As an only child, the intense concentration of self is the norm; it is not a state that I find frightening or, in any way, unusual. To find oneself in the terrifying situations that both Pip or Ginger encounters, I can imagine experiencing feelings of fear and helplessness and desperation, but not necessarily loneliness. Any nascent propensity for loneliness that I might have experienced in youth was quickly diverted by reading. Reading is a solitary activity but, for me, it is also a pathway into a world, richly populated by countless others: characters, whose stories are waiting to be discovered; the protagonist—Biggles—who is the focus of the story; the antagonist—von Stalhein—who is the villain of the piece; the deuteragonist—Algy—who is the secondary lead; the love interest—the Supermarine Spitfire—who provides an object of desire for the protagonist; all the tertiary characters—Tex and Taffy and Smyth and Ferocity—who populate the background; and then, more intimately, the author, who invites you to analyse the workings of their mind and how it displays itself on the printed page. Too many books in the world to be lonely. Too few hours to read them all.

I wonder if W. E. Johns ever read *Moby Dick*? I imagine it quite likely. For some reason, Biggles' fellow officers at 266 Squadron—McLaren and Mahoney—always put me in mind of the similarly alliterative pairing of Starbuck and Stubbs, first and second mate respectively, battling the high seas together aboard *Pequod.*

Reading #13: *Biggles – Charter Pilot*

Biggles and dinosaurs. When I was a boy, if I were to have been asked what two things I was most passionate about, I would have answered, without hesitation: dinosaurs and Biggles. Or, I might have said: Biggles and dinosaurs. Ask me what I am passionate about today and I might have added a few other items to the list but, rest assured, dinosaurs and Biggles will still feature in there somewhere. We're back to those Jesuits again: "Give me the child for the first seven years, and I will give you the man."

The Jesuit reference is not without relevance: descendants of Jesuits feature in the Biggles short story *The Adventure of the Horticultural Hermits*, published in the collection of short stories *Biggles – Charter Pilot* (Oxford, 1943).

I can vividly recall the first time that I read *Biggles – Charter Pilot*. I would have been twelve years old; the new-look Armada paperback had just been issued (see *Biggles Rebranded*); the OUP first edition remained/s a rarity, and one only recently acquired.

Biggles – Charter Pilot contains sixteen short stories. The stories are told by Ginger to his comrades in Number 666 (Fighter) Squadron during lulls in the hostilities during the Second World War, and they recall past adventures of Biggles, Algy and Ginger in the company of the eccentric Dr Augustus Duck in exotic locations around the world, from Nicaragua (*The Adventure of the Purple Cloud*) to Australia (*The Adventure of the Haunted Creek*); from the furthermost tip of South America (*The Adventure of the Patagonian Giants*) to the icy wastes of Greenland (*The Adventure of the Musty Mammoth*).

Dr Augustus Duck is introduced as a biologist, who is interested in investigating reports of unusual phenomena—a pursuit with which I am much in sympathy—and, in *Biggles – Charter Pilot*, our eponymous hero and his companions find themselves flung into wild escapades in which they encounter, amongst other creatures, prehistoric pterodactyls, dodos and a giant woolly mammoth.

Dinosaurs and Biggles. My two passions colliding head-on. It should have been a marriage made in heaven. It was not. My twelve-year old self was outraged.

Of course, this had not been the first time that Biggles had strayed somewhat into the realms of fantasy: *Biggles Hits the Trail* features a mysterious death ray, carnivorous centipedes, and a magic mountain that glowed blue, all of which I had lapped up with unbridled enjoyment. With *Biggles Hits the Trail* I was prepared to suspend disbelief and just enjoy the story. *Biggles – Charter Pilot* was different. It ventured too closely into personal territory; it danced too liberally on the boundary between make-believe and science.

Admittedly, in most cases, W. E. Johns offered up a rational, scientific explanation for the strange phenomena, which Biggles and his crew encounter during their dalliances with Dr Duck, but there were sufficient loose ends to leave a critical twelve-year old incensed. It felt like Johns had taken my two passions and was being disrespectful to them both.

It has taken me a long time to return to *Biggles – Charter Pilot*. Those early impressions are not ones, which can be easily dismissed. However, in a spirit of *entente cordiale*, I have gone back to the book. As an adult, I can read the stories with a different mind-set. Now I can appreciate and enjoy the stories by picturing them as somehow separate from the wider Biggles canon. Nevertheless, the book remains an anomaly.

To better understand the book, it is perhaps necessary to place it in the context of its time. The opening story—*The Adventure of the Enchanted Island*—in which Biggles encounters a giant crab on an unexplored island, was first published in October 1941 in the *Boy's Own Paper*. At that time, Britain had been embroiled in the Second World War for two full years, and things were not looking particularly rosy. On the Eastern Front, Operation Barbarossa had commenced and German troops were pushing into Russia; despite the Blitz being over, bombs were still regularly falling on London; the Japanese attack on Pearl Harbour was still two months in the future, meaning that in many theatres of war Britain was standing alone, the Americans yet to enter the conflict; it was a period of great uncertainty, when it would have been hard to be optimistic about the future of Europe. Even Biggles, who, up until that point, had chiefly only ever known victory in his encounters against a German foe, would have been hard-pressed to find any crumbs of comfort listening to news emanating from the Front. In that climate, a retreat into escapism must have been a preferable alternative to reflecting the grim reality of the times.

Rationally, I can read *Biggles - Charter Pilot* in this context but, emotionally, my twelve-year old self will not be so easily silenced. How can I assimilate *Biggles – Charter Pilot* into the Biggles world order? If it were an episode of a soap opera, *Biggles – Charter Pilot* could be explained away as nothing more than a fantastic dream, with Biggles emerging out of a shower in the final chapter. But that won't do. It would be nice to think that Ginger was simply spinning some tall tales to entertain his fellow pilots but, if there is one quality that marks out Ginger, it is his straight-forward, guileless honesty. No good looking for explanations down that route. So, how am I left?

For me, *Biggles - Charter Pilot* will remain an eternally ugly duckling. And, no doubt if Dr Augustus Duck is investigating the phenomenon, it will be a *giant* ugly duckling at that.

My Lost World

When I was not receiving worthy volumes of illustrated Bible stories for my Christmas presents (see *The Best Christmas Present*), I was sometimes fortunate enough to be given a big book about dinosaurs, full of colour pictures and pull-out timelines from the Precambrian to the Holocene. The names of some of the time periods were particularly evocative: Devonian; Silurian; Ordovician. They sounded like mystical races straight out of Dr Who. However, for someone primarily interested in dinosaurs, the most crucial periods were the Triassic, and the Jurassic and the Cretaceous, when the big critters ruled supreme.

Dinosaurs provided the perfect fuel for a boy blessed—cursed?—with an overactive imagination. They also fulfilled a vital role to satisfy that nerdish desire to create lists (see *The Naming of Parts*). Alongside the natural list of the geological time zones could be added a list of each of the dinosaurs that existed during each of those periods. And the dinosaurs all had such long and complicated names, which it was a task to learn, a feat to pronounce, a challenge to spell—screw you archaeopteryx, the missing link in an age before spell-check—and a priggish delight to be able to show off about. However, like so much of the stuff you learn when you are a child, it is not until you are an adult that you realise that most of it was wrong. In many ways, children should be thankful that they attain such a level of enlightenment to realise this fact; as adults, I am equally convinced that almost everything we learn is also wrong, except that there is no longer anyone there to tell us otherwise, so we remain in a perpetual ignorance of our own common incompetence. I do still find myself feeling protective of the dinosaurs that I learned about as a child, though. I've got no great empathy with the Velociraptors and Dilophosaurus of *Jurassic Park* vintage; my allegiance is with the club-tailed Ankylosaurus and the sail-finned Dimetrodon, who featured in my picture books when I was young. And as for the whole Brontosaurus versus Apatosaurus debate, I am firmly old-skool: Brontosaurus all the way.

An ambition I held as a child was to visit the dinosaurs in Crystal Palace Park. These were, of course, not real dinosaurs, but palaeontological statues, which date from the Victorian period, and feature representations of Iguanodons, Megalosaurus, plesiosaurs and ichthyosaurs. I never did visit the statues as a child. Did I visit them as an adult? I'm not sure. I can picture myself visiting them; I can see myself walking along the pathways in Crystal Palace Park, spotting the various sculptures in the undergrowth; I even wrote an account of going there. But did I actually go? I'm still not sure. My wife says that we never went; my son says that we never went; unusually, I have no photographic evidence to show that I ever went. So, what is going on? Is my family collectively gaslighting me? Am I experiencing another case of false memory syndrome? Or has my imagination returned to the idea of visiting the dinosaurs for so long that it has crystalized into a physical reality? Shades of Rupert Sheldrake's theories on morphic resonance and formative causation. Crystal Palace Park is my lost world, eternally caught in a netherworld between fact and fiction.

Sir Arthur Conan Doyle's *The Lost World* is indisputably pure fiction but was a seminal book for me. The possibility that dinosaurs might still exist, tucked away in a forgotten, inaccessible corner of the planet, hidden away from Man, has been an enduring—if increasingly forlorn—hope. And whilst discoveries of previously 'unknown' creatures continue to happen each year; and even when such a large creature as the okapi was only discovered as late as 1901, the chances of the existence of a lost world, as described by Conan Doyle remain a fantasy. The location that Conan Doyle chose for his own hidden kingdom was the top of one of the distinctive table-top mountains, or *tepuis* in Venezuela: Mount Roraima. For many years, I fostered a wish to visit the location myself; but the years roll by, the destination does not get any easier to get to; and I have begun to more enjoy being pampered in luxury hotels in Italy than hiking for several weeks in the sweating heat of the Amazon biome. And so, in my place, I would love to send Biggles instead, to act as my proxy. Age does not wither him, and I am sure that he would relish the challenge. I might have to wait another few years until the Biggles books fall out of copyright before I can write it—W. E. Johns died in 1968, and copyright lasts for seventy years after the death of the author. So, 2038. I will be 71 years old myself by then. *Biggles in the Lost World.* You read about it here first.

Mary Anning and Joan Worralson

Before either Bikini Kill or the Spice Girls had been credited with inventing the phrase, two trailblazers for 'girl power' were Mary Anning and Joan Worralson. One of them I could publicly acknowledge and exalt her virtues and achievements; the other, I could not.

Mary Anning was something of a hero for me even if, when I was very young, I sometimes muddled her up with Grace Darling; I think they must have both been part of the same Brooke Bond Tea Cards series. Putting aside *The Piccolo Encyclopedia of Useful Facts* (see *The Naming of Parts*), the Brooke Bond Tea Cards were one of my most fruitful sources of factual information. Mary Anning lived in Lyme Regis and, in the early decades of the nineteenth century, made her living as a fossil hunter along the stretch of cliffs on the south coast of Dorset, which we now call the Jurassic Coast. Amongst a huge number of fossil finds, she was responsible for finding the first correctly identified ichthyosaur skeleton, which went on to be displayed at the Natural History Museum in London; the first pterosaur skeleton in the UK; and several plesiosaur skeletons, and the discoveries she made formed crucial evidence for the theory of the extinction of species, an idea that was not widely believed at the time. Many of the discoveries she made, she did so whilst still a child; a fact that had a particular resonance for me at a comparable age. I was proud of Mary Anning; felt a kinship with her through a shared youthfulness and interests; aspired to emulate her achievements. But, I could not admit to a similar connection with Joan Worralson.

By way of an over-simplified introduction, Joan Worralson is Biggles' female counterpart. W. E. Johns wrote his first 'Worrals' book, *Worrals of the WAAF*, in 1941, going on to write a further ten novels featuring the female aviator. Six of these books, Johns wrote between the years 1941 and 1945, meaning that Worrals was almost as ubiquitous during the War years as was Biggles himself. The War years also saw the arrival of another Johns' creation, the Commando officer, Captain Lorrington King, more widely known as 'Gimlet'. Two Gimlet books were published during the War—*King of the Commandos* and *Gimlet Goes Again*—with a further eight titles to follow, not including the anthology *Comrades in Arms*, which includes stories featuring Biggles, Gimlet and Worrals. Gimlet's creation had as much to do with army recruitment as it did with literary inspiration; Biggles and Worrals had encouraged so many young people to join the air services, it was hoped that a youthful commando hero might provoke a similar positive impetus towards the army.

The problem with Worrals was that they were 'girls' books. They fell into the same category as the Chalet School novels by Elinor Brent-Dyer or the Pony Club stories by Christine and Josephine Pullein-Thompson. As far as novels for boys and novels for girls were concerned, there was little crossover. The Worrals books also suffered by not being reprinted in paperback in the same way that the Biggles books were and, by the seventies and eighties, they had disappeared from most bookshops' shelves. Regardless of that fact, though, my nascent machismo would not have permitted me to be seen reading them. Thank goodness, then, that I am not so troubled by the rigidity of gender classifications in adulthood. I have been able to make up for my childhood shortcomings and add the Worrals books to my literary canon, which has been a bigger positive for me than I suspect it has been for her.

W. E. Johns, himself, was something of a champion for the role of women in aviation, and in creating stories that showed Worrals, along with her friend Betty 'Frecks' Lovell, battling against, and conquering, the ingrained chauvinism of the military establishment in their roles as flying officers in the Women's Auxiliary Air Force, he created a little-known feminist icon, who was ahead of her times, fighting prejudice and discrimination: "'Miss Worralson,' he said bitingly, 'if and when it is decided to teach young women to fly fighting aeroplanes—and for the sake of everyone else in the sky I hope that time is not yet—you will receive your orders from me.'" (*Worrals of the WAAF*).

Although female characters are rather few and far between in the Biggles books—these were 'boys' stories after all—when these characters do appear they do not take the classic adventure-story roles of 'submissive woman waiting to be rescued' but, instead, tend to be strong, independent characters in their own right. In *Biggles in the South Seas*, the young Polynesian girl Full Moon is shown to be someone in complete mastery of her surroundings, saving Ginger time and time again, on land, sea and–

in the treetops—air: "Ginger could only admire the efficiency with which she went about a task which would have made many experienced sailors pause." (*Biggles in the South Seas*, p. 164); "Ginger could never have got to the machine unaided… but Full Moon came to his assistance and made him put his hand on her shoulder." (*Biggles in the South Seas*, p. 81); "'Me swim down… I cut rope, but reckon you die plenty quick, so I pull you on reef.'" (*Biggles in the South Seas*, p. 213).

Similarly, neither the Principessa Marietta Loretto de Palma, nor Jeanette and Madame Ducoste, in *Biggles Fails to Return* Hodder, 1943), are mere bystanders in the story. Instead, they are all active and committed participants in the French Resistance against the occupation of their country, and this despite Bertie's assertion that: "'Women and planes don't mix.'" (*Biggles Fails to Return*, p. 180).

Both Mary Anning and Joan Worralson have had something of a revival in recent years with, in my opinion, mixed results. Joan Worralson found a temporary new publisher in IndieBooks, who reissued three of her earliest adventures, *Worrals of the WAAF*, *Worrals Carries On* and *Worrals Flies Again,* all benefitting from contemporary illustrations by Matt Kindt.

Mary Anning's life story has been brought to the big screen in the movie *Ammonite*, starring Kate Winslet as Mary and Saoise Ronan as her friend Charlotte Murchison. So far, so good. However, in a piece of silver-screen sensationalism, a lesbian love-story is contrived between the two leading protagonists, which has entirely no basis in recorded fact. The unexpurgated story of Mary Anning's life is extraordinary enough; it seems like a cheap debasement of her achievements in the field of palaeontology to trivialise them by creating a romantic fiction.

Who would have thought that in an age supposedly more committed to gender equality that it is W. E. Johns who displays the superior feminist credentials.

The Importance of Myths

Whilst the chances of me visiting Mount Roraima remained low (see *My Lost World*), the possibility of travelling to Loch Ness seemed entirely feasible to my teenage self. If I couldn't see Professor Challenger's dinosaurs in Venezuela; I could surely spot the fabled Monster in Scotland.

During my childhood, Nessie was relatively ubiquitous. New photographs were routinely published; old photographs were regularly reshown; Tim Dinsdale's book—*Loch Ness Monster*—which was originally published by RKP in 1961 received a Target paperback reissue as *The Story of the Loch Ness Monster*, reaching a wider audience.

Statistically, the 1960s represented the heyday for Nessie sightings and, before that, the 1930s. At those times, public interest in the monster was at its peak. Yearly sightings would frequently number in the twenties. The last 'peak' year for sightings was 1996, with seventeen recorded encounters; with 2017 a relatively vintage year for this Millennium with eight 'official' sightings. However, the trend is clear. Nessie is on the wane. If this current direction continues, she'll soon be in imminent danger of extinction.

So, what is happening?

I think that it is no coincidence that 1996, the last year which recorded multiple sightings of the Loch Ness Monster corresponds fairly closely with the start of widespread public access to the internet.

Each generation needs its own myths. Myths serve as a mirror of prevailing social circumstances, as well as a driver for their formation, and the times they are a changing.

The internet has served a dual death-blow to Nessie. On the one hand, it provides an easily-available source of tested scientific information, which is quickly able to dispel some of the more fanciful claims, which have surrounded the existence of the monster; on the other hand, it offers up a vast array of new myths, many of which are manufactured either for profit or publicity, and which perhaps more accurately reflect the rapidly changing, short-attention span, consumerist society in which we now live.

A YouTube-savvy generation is neither gratified nor satisfied by grainy images of a minor disturbance in the pattern of waves across a cold and distant loch. It wants its monster myths to be performing handstands on skateboards; or shaking hands with the President on the front lawn of the White House.

And it is not just poor old Nessie. Popular interest in the Yeti also appears at an all-time low. Back in 1954, the *Daily Mail* sponsored an expedition to travel to Everest and Kanchenjunga with the intention of ascertaining definitive proof of the existence of the Yeti. The mission was called the Snowman Expedition and was led by notable mountaineer John Angelo Jackson. The *Daily Mail* expedition followed closely in the 'footsteps' of Eric Shipton's 1951 Everest expedition, which returned with intriguing stories of having discovered unexplained tracks in the snows of the high Himalayas, and it was they who took the classic photograph of an enormous footprint in the snow, pictured next to an ice-axe for scale. The Yeti was quickly assimilated into popular children's culture. Hergé's *Tintin in Tibet* was published in 1960 and two complete storylines of Doctor Who, produced during the excellent Patrick Troughton's era as the second Doctor—*The Abominable Snowman* (1967) and *The Web of Fear* (1968)—featured robotic Yetis as the principal baddie. But, like Nessie, social media has dealt the Yeti a side-swipe, from which it may never recover. And Big Foot? Not much mention of him/her for a while either. As Biggles himself observed: "'The trouble with the world today is nobody believes in anything any more.'" (*Biggles Looks Back*, p. 77).

No doubt Dr Augustus Duck would have happily set Biggles, Algy and Ginger on the tracks of some of these mythical beasts but, in some cases, what is more important is the continuation of the myth rather than a logical explanation, which ultimately dispels it. It is this same status quo that sustains most of the world's organised religions.

In the case of Nessie, it looks as though it might be public apathy rather than solid scientific evidence, which will result in its extinction. And, against that, there is no protection.

Reading #14: *Biggles in the Jungle*

There is more than an element of vanity in my inclusion of *Biggles in the Jungle* (Oxford, 1942) amongst my selection of the Biggles books to include in this volume. After all, it is not up there with my absolute favourite Biggles titles. Indeed, along with *Biggles in the South Seas* (Oxford, 1940), it is something of a chronological anomaly, in as much as they were both written during wartime, but both relate stories, which it would have to be presumed are supposed to have occurred either prior to the outbreak of the Second World War, or as part of some kind of alternative history where the Second World War never took place at all. In this respect, *Biggles in the Jungle* is a particularly interesting example. The first page of the book sees Biggles referred to as Squadron-Leader Bigglesworth, his wartime title, and a map that appears in the book is dated 1937. However, Biggles refers to their current adventure as "a pleasure cruise, with no particular object in view beyond seeing something of the world." (p. 8). A trip suggested by Ginger who had been "bored by a spell of inactivity." (p. 8). Hardly, an appropriate description of the turbulent years leading up to the start of the Second World War.

Biggles in the Jungle takes Biggles, Algy and Ginger to British Honduras, now Belize. W. E. Johns returns to this destination for one of his Gimlet books: *Gimlet Off the Map* (Brockhampton, 1951). It is a small country in Central America, bordered by Guatemala to the south and west, the Quintana Roo state of Mexico to the north, and the Caribbean Sea to the east. Blessed with a magnificent coastal coral reef and numerous offshore islands; vast tracts of subtropical jungle and rainforest; and pine-covered mountains, it is home to a rich profusion of animals, birds, reptiles and plant life, making it a biodiversity hotspot. Added to its natural wonders, Belize is also the location of a number of historically-important pre-Columbian Maya archaeological sites. The Maya flourished in Belize from 2000BCE until the Spanish conquest of Central America in the 16th century, reaching the peak of its civilisation between 300 and 900CE. Many of their ancient cities have already been excavated, whilst many more lie waiting to be discovered, buried deep in the luxuriant forest. But, enough of my free advertising campaign for the Belize Tourist Board. During my late-twenties, I was fortunate enough to spend a considerable period of time in Belize, and I think this simple fact alone thoroughly justifies me in being able to include an author photo, taken in Placencia in the south of Belize, at a time when I could still display cool shades, a healthy tan and something halfway to approaching a ripped six-pack.

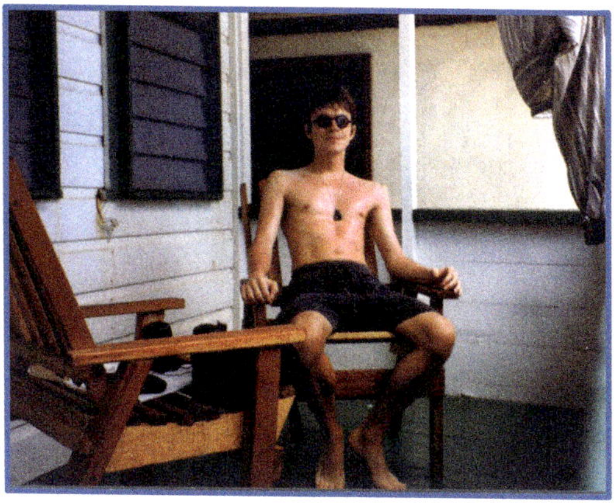

Vanity of vanities! All is vanity. And what does vanity mean in a book written by W. E. Johns? Why, the villain of the piece, of course. And by way of a natural segue, there is a good example of one of Johns' vain villains tucked away deep into the depths of *Biggles in the Jungle*. Vain in his attire, vain in his self-appointed title, the King of the Forest is described thus: "He was dressed—or rather, over-dressed—in a uniform so elaborate, so heavy with gold braid, and of colours so brilliant that not even a cinema commissionaire would have dared to wear it." (p. 74). Similarly, in *Biggles Flies West* and *No Rest for Biggles* (Hodder, 1956), a baddie's propensity for being over-ostentatious in terms of sartorial attire is quickly ridiculed by Johns: "…wearing a uniform so elaborate that in different circumstances he might have cut a comical figure." (*Biggles Flies West*, p. 133); "…plastering himself in gold braid like his aide-de-camp." (*No Rest for Biggles*, p. 33). With perhaps the most extreme example occurring in *Biggles in the Blue* (Brockhampton, 1953): "…beautifully-pressed lilac trousers tapered almost to a point at the ankles, and a square-shouldered, wasp-waisted jacket with long lapels… a flaunting red tie decorated with dice, and a large gold pin, completed an outfit that would have been ridiculous had not the man, who was tall and slim, walked with the smooth grace of a panther." (*Biggles in the Blue*, p. 44). It is interesting, too, that all of these "…overdressed popinjays" (*No Rest for Biggles*, p. 27) are black men. Mildred has been conspicuously quiet for some time now—have I missed her? Not noticeably—but I fear that she might have something to say about this. Noteworthy, too, is the fact that the 'bad' white men in *Biggles in the Jungle* all suffer from jaundice, which turns their complexion from white to yellow: "…a tall, emaciated-looking man whose skin, yellow from recurrent bouts of fever, seemed to be drawn tightly over the bones." (p. 38) and "…he could only be called white by courtesy, for jaundice had set its mark on his face, leaving it an unhealthy yellow." (p. 77). However, for anyone beginning to side with Mildred's opinions regarding the accusations of racism, which have been levelled against Johns, I would first advise them to refer to Peter Berresford Ellis and Piers Williams' excellent *By Jove, Biggles!* where the authors provide a breakdown of the ethnicity of every Biggles' villain across the entire oeuvre of the series, an astonishing achievement (see pp 238-239 *By Jove, Biggles!*). It is not just black men with whom Johns links vanity and immorality. Other signs of a disreputable individual are ostentatious displays of wealth, overly-quaffed hair and a liberal use of pomade: "Fairly studded with diamonds, and reeks like a chemist's shop of scent and hair oil—makes you sick." (*Biggles Hunts Big Game*, p. 180). Johns is also critical of pretentious titles and pomposity. I wonder if this is linked to his own clashes with authority, particularly prior to the start of the Second World War when he was critical of many of the British government's policies regarding defence; and, frequently within the Biggles books, the 'Top Brass' are referred to in less-than-complimentary terms, their own failings and vanities displayed for all to see in the 'scrambled eggs'—gold braid—that they wear on their caps and lapels.

If I may be permitted one further vanity myself—this time the ability to correct a statement within the book (see *The Power of Humour*)—I should point out that although Johns states that the ancient Mayan cities of Tikal and Uaxactun are in Belize, they are both actually in Guatemala, although both lie no great distance from the town of San Ignacio in Cayo District, close to Belize's western border. However, Johns does manage to cover his back regarding this rare lapse by declaring that "as in the case of most countries in tropical America, the frontier was assumed to be somewhere in the forest, but it was not possible to say precisely where." (p. 19). One aspect of the country in which Johns was entirely accurate, though, was in his description of their extensive network of caves: "It seemed to go on interminably, but then suddenly opened out into a tremendous cavity in the earth, not unlike a cathedral." (p. 181). Millions of years ago, during the formation of the Maya Mountains in the centre of the country, a large area of limestone was uplifted, which has subsequently eroded by the actions of water to form a vast system of caves, including Chiquibul, which includes one of the single largest underground chambers in the world.

And, to end, an anecdote. I was interested to see that in *Biggles in the Jungle*, Ginger, ever one for embarking on a new hobby, becomes interested in insects: "As a form of relaxation on the ground he had decide to collect butterflies, the beauty of which at some of their ports of call had entranced him, with the result that he was taking a new interest in entomology." (p. 9). On the same page, Ginger also reveals that he only knows the name Honduras because "I once saw the name on a postage stamp, otherwise I shouldn't have known that the place existed." (p. 9). It was the juxtaposition of these two seemingly disparate sentences that brought to mind the following event.

On my very first visit to Belize, I was drinking a cool Belikin beer at the *al fresco* bar of Blancaneaux Lodge, on the banks of Privassion Creek. A fellow bar habitué, an elderly Englishman, dressed in a colonial-style white safari jacket, was carefully studying a sheet of colourful Belizean stamps that had recently been issued. There were twelve stamps all together, ranging in price from five cents to ten Belizean dollars, and they depicted a range of Belizean insect life, including Tarantula Wasps, Peanut-head Bugs and Coconut Weevils.

"Ever seen one of those ugly blighters?" he asked, pointing to the ten cents stamp, upon which was depicted a Harlequin Beetle.

In an act of perfect synchronicity, and without me having to utter a word, the very critter itself chose that moment to emerge from where it had been hiding in his top jacket pocket.

The Crystal Skull

Throughout life, there are certain experiences and events, which on the surface may appear to have no discernible effect on an individual but which, at a deeper, unconscious level, have a profound influence in shaping that individual's future thinking. *Arthur C. Clarke's Mysterious World* was one such event for me.

The concept of *Arthur C. Clarke's Mysterious World* was to take a scientific lens to instances of unexplained phenomena from around the world. The programme had a grading system for the different kinds of mysteries it investigated: Mysteries of the First Kind were defined as those that had puzzled our ancestors, but which through modern scientific advances we could now fully explain; Mysteries of the Second Kind were mysteries that still held a certain puzzlement for us, but where science had suggested possible solutions; and Mysteries of the Third Kind were ones where, frankly, no one had an effing clue.

Although the programme was attributed to ACC, the famous science fiction writer only actually appeared briefly at the beginning and end of each episode, speaking from his home in Sri Lanka, usually providing an optimistic introduction and a balanced conclusion to each broadcast. ACC was a great advocate of scientific advancement, particularly in the field of space exploration, but even he was apt to be sceptical of certain mysteries: I recall he only gave the poor old Sasquatch a 10% chance of existence. Pretty generous odds, IMHO.

The teenage me lapped up each episode, enthralled. It seems extraordinary now to realise that the running time of each show was only half an hour in duration (shown on ITV, that running time included adverts as well). In my memory, it seemed as though the programme lasted the entire evening; such was both its significance for me and, also, the length of time I spent afterwards lost in contemplative reflection of its content.

Back then, the shows that had me most gripped were, perhaps predictably, the ones, which featured unexplained beasts of myth and legends: Nessie; the Yeti; the Mokèlé-mbèmbé. If juvenile will-power alone could have summoned these legendary cryptids into life, then they would have all existed in abundance.

The opening title sequence for each episode featured prominently one of the strange crystal skulls that, at the time, were a puzzle and wonderment to science. The most famous crystal skull ever to be 'discovered' was reputedly unearthed from the Lubaantun Maya ruins in the Toledo district of southern Belize, close to the town of Punta Gorda. Originally reputed to be of pre-Columbian Mesoamerican origin, the skulls have since been revealed to have been manufactured in Germany sometime in the mid-19th century.

One other episode, though, is a teenage standout: *Out of the Blue*. The episode featured a phenomenon that Clarke classified at the time as a Mystery of the Third Kind. The phenomenon was frogs raining from the sky. Of course, these days, we have a scientifically-proven, rational explanation for the bizarre event—tornadic waterspouts can carry fish and frogs for several miles in the atmosphere before depositing them as a form of rain. Nevertheless, such was the show's power that I still always make a close scrutiny of the heavens for low-flying amphibians before venturing out.

It might seem peculiar that the show still holds such affection for me when many of its so-called mysteries have since been explained and, with them, the destruction of many of my childhood beliefs, but I am a firm believer that we can't know how much we know until we know how little we know.

Teenage Rage

Richard was a friend from my junior school days, until his family moved to Bristol and I never heard from him again. However, before that monumental event, I was a regular visitor to Richard's house, where his mum would ply us with—extremely alcoholic—chocolate-covered rum truffles, and I would stand for hours in front of a wall in his back dining-room, admiring his dad's fish-tanks.

It was a dark room, and the tanks were darker still and, rather than being composed of one large aquarium, they were a hotchpotch of lots of little tanks, all piled one on top of one another, with numerous mechanical pumps whirring, sending up streams of bubbles, reflecting the dim light. As far as I could see, most of the tanks appeared to be empty, or simply contained the detritus of a past fish life, but several of the tanks contained specimens of the same, similar-looking fish; a watchful, black-eyed fish, with a rather mournful-looking downturned mouth, chubby body and red underside.

"Why do you keep them in separate tanks?" I asked.

"Because they will eat each other," came back the reply.

They didn't look as though they would eat each other. They appeared rather slow-moving fish. I stuck another rum truffle into my mouth and pressed my nose closer to the glass.

"Watch."

My friend introduced some feed into each of the tanks. There was a blur of movement, which was too swift to follow and then, in a fashion reminiscent of Gene Wilder's depiction of The Waco Kid in *Blazing Saddles*, by the time I looked again the fish had returned to their slow-moving, dead-eyed positions, as though nothing had happened.

"See that?"

"No," I answered, truthfully.

"That's piranhas for you. Can reduce a man to a skeleton in under five minutes."

I withdrew my nose from the glass of their aquarium and, still sucking my rum truffle, observed the small fish rather more thoughtfully.

It seemed that as well as all the humans that had to be feared during the 1970s (see *The Gold Hind and Glue Sniffing*) there were plenty of other critters to be feared, too, and, in *Biggles in the Jungle*, W. E. Johns manages to reference them all, even if, in a few instances, they are geographically out of place.

The small fish in my friend's fish tank were, of course, piranhas. Remember, this was still the 1970s; the Dangerous Wild Animals Act did not come into law until 1976; before that if you wanted to keep a tiger in your bedroom you were pretty much free to do so; in comparison, piranhas were relatively small fry. Biggles describes the fish: "'Man-eating fish,' explained Biggles. 'They're not very big, but they're the most voracious creatures in the world.'" (*Biggles in the Jungle*, p. 97). Typically, piranhas are found in tropical freshwater rivers in South America, not in Belize, although their invasive cousin, the Pacu, has been discovered in some Belizean rivers. The poor piranha's reputation was not helped by the release in 1978 of the comedy horror film *Piranha*, which was a low-budget version of *Jaws.*

Another geographical anomaly in *Biggles in the Jungle* is the appearance of an anaconda. Once again, this is a creature more abundant in South America, particularly the Orinoco Basin, not Belize, despite the fact that one Belizean eco lodge famously posted a very convincing April Fool's picture of one swimming in a pool in their grounds.

However, two scary creatures that Belize is home to, and which Johns describes to great effects are swarms of army ants, and big, black tarantula spiders. There is a terrifying understatement in local chicle-collector Dusky's assertion: "'De ants are coming.'" (*Biggles in the Jungle*, p. 99). However, W. E. Johns perhaps misses a trick or two regarding a few real-life Belizean denizens that he could have included. There is the fer-de-lance, a pit viper, which has been known to attack humans, and which Johns is all too familiar with: "The brutes are about six feet long, greyish-brown in colour, with dark cross-bands edged with yellowish-green." (*Biggles in the Blue*, pp 59-60); the poison dart frog, which secretes a toxic venom; the vampire bat, which can be a carrier of dangerous bacteria and viruses; the Portuguese man o' war jellyfish, which has a sting powerful enough to paralyse and kill; and the, sadly, now ubiquitous lionfish, an invasive species, which has venomous spines along its back. Bang goes that job working for the Belize Tourist Board.

Biggles' encounters with wild beasts can always be relied upon to produce an episode of great excitement and, although Biggles might sometimes be guilty of despatching a few endangered species to the great hereafter in order to save his own skin, for the most part his attitude towards wild animals is one of respect, rather than enmity; it is invariably the 'human' animals who are the greater villains of the piece.

However, scary as were all these creatures, I could rationalise my fears by thinking that they were far away. But, there was one fear that was dangerously close at hand, scarcely kept at bay by a watchful border force and a strict quarantine law. Growing up in the UK in the 1970s, there was one threat above all others, which preyed upon the fears of the public consciousness. It was not the possibility of nuclear meltdown; it was not HIV—too early for that; it was not even the moral disintegration of society in the face of a potty-mouthed punk revolution. No, what most scared every red-blooded Englishman was rabies.

There were fierce quarantine rules protecting the country. No animal could arrive on these shores without first being caged for six months. It was only the fact that we were an island nation that meant we hadn't been overrun already. Everyone believed that every four-legged critter on the mainland of Europe was infected; a carrier at best. It had been part of the reason for public resistance to joining the EU in 1973 and to form closer ties in 1985; perhaps it was still in the minds of Leave voters during the Brexit referendum in 2016? Similar to the prospective invasion of our green and pleasant land in 1940 by Operation Sealion, in the 1970s it seemed as though we were only a Channel's width away from a rabies-led Armageddon.

The media fuelled this anxiety. Every incidence of rabies was recorded in the popular press in graphic detail. It was scarcely possible to turn on the TV without tuning into a government health warning or public information film about the risks of travelling to the continent. My first ever trip abroad—to Calais aged 8—was entirely spoilt by the constant fear that I would be licked/chased/bitten by a demented rabid beast. And the disease became the subject of several popular paperback novels—*Saliva* by

Walter Harris (Star, 1977) and *The Rage* by Jack Ramsey (Sphere, 1977).

The culmination of all this hysteria was a BBC Scotland mini-series aired in 1983, called *The Mad Death.* My memories of this series are hazy at best, but I have recollections of a frothy-mouthed feral fox hurling itself maniacally at the windscreen of a car, leaving a slimy residue of presumably festering contagious germs, waiting to infect the unwary, and also memories of the hallucinatory dream sequences of the infected victims, which seemed to involve a surprising amount of naked flesh and eroticism for a primetime show.

But then all the anxiety seemed to stop. Did rabies simply just go away? Or is it just that we have even scarier things to worry about these days?

Reading #15: *Biggles' Second Case*

"Well, chaps, I think that's all." In typical Biggles understatement, that is his assessment of the end of the Second World War (*Sergeant Bigglesworth CID*, p.3). And, although the War has been over for three years by the time that *Biggles' Second Case* is published in 1948, the War's influence is still very much in evidence in the plot of the book. In attempting to track down the rogue U-boat U-517 commanded by Captain Ulrich von Schonbeck, Biggles finds himself pitted against a Nazi who believes: "'For some of us the war will never be over.'" (p. 96). And, of course, for many combatants, the War did not end in 1945. Perhaps most famous amongst these were the Japanese holdouts, soldiers who would either not believe the fact of the Japanese surrender, or who had become stranded on such remote outposts of the South Pacific that they simply never received communication that the War had ended. Into the 1950s it was still possible to find groups of Japanese soldiers pursuing their own private hostilities; and the last two confirmed holdouts were not discovered until as late as 1974, almost thirty years after the War had officially ended. Hiroo Onoda only surrendered on the island of Lubang in March 1974 after his old commanding officer relieved him of duty; and Teruo Nakamura became the longest known holdout when he surrendered in December 1974 on Morotai in Indonesia's Maluku Islands. A Japanese holdout plays an important part in the plot of *Biggles and the Lost Sovereigns* (Brockhampton, 1964): "After the war a lot of Japanese troops in Borneo, and the islands of what were then the Dutch East Indies, refused to surrender, being convinced they'd be shot." (*Biggles and the Lost Sovereigns*, p. 163). The book was published in 1964, so it was at a time when holdouts were still being discovered on Guam, and neighbouring islands.

Of course, many Nazis managed to flee Germany prior to the end of the Second World War, some escaping to South America, amongst them high-ranking officers such as Adolf Eichmann and Josef Mengele. Conspiracy theories, alternative histories and fictions about resurgent Nazi plots continue to exert a certain fascination in popular culture, the most famous example perhaps being Ira Levin's 1976 thriller novel *The Boys from Brazil,* later filmed starring Gregory Peck and Laurence Olivier.

However, in *Biggles' Second Case*, the Nazi von Schonbeck's motives are not ideological ones, but ones of personal greed. Biggles is called in to investigate in his capacity as an air detective working for Scotland Yard, a role that he will continue to fulfil for the remainder of the series of books, alongside long-standing companions Algy, Ginger and Bertie.

Needless to say, von Schonbeck ultimately receives his just desserts: W. E. Johns is consistently even-handed in applying the philosophy of 'what goes around comes around'. He is an unwitting observer of Karma, before the term ever became fashionable. Without wanting to entirely spoil the ending of the book, I could perhaps paraphrase von Schonbeck's demise in the fashion of Humbert Humbert's description of his parents' death in Vladimir Nabokov's *Lolita*: "Running comma bog". From a child, I have always had a healthy respect for the dangers of quicksand; it must have either originated here, or from reading *The Hound of the Baskervilles* by Arthur Conan Doyle. Careful never to put myself in a position of peril from this deadly hazard, my one lapse came during a long walk in the Nephin Beg range of mountains of County Mayo in western Ireland. I was following the famous drover's path from Newport to Bangor Erris, a distance of some twenty-four miles, in a region reputed to be amongst the most isolated in the whole of Europe. The route circumvented the infamous Owenduff blanket bog. We were a small party of walkers and, despite the day starting rainy, it was in high spirits that we set out on our trek. Along the route there were several small rivers that had to be crossed and, although the high peaks of the mountains—Slieve Carr and Nephin—were constant companions, the route never climbed so high as to feel arduous. Several ruins of old stone dwellings were passed; not a single other person was sighted, except for an otherworldly party of three horse traders, leading a black horse and followed by two dogs, which looked as though it had stepped out of a different century.

In the end, it was not me who fell foul of the landscape, but one of my companions. Always slightly behind the group, Enid was suddenly not there. We discovered her, beyond waist deep, submerged in a sphagnum bog, from which she was incapable of escaping by her own means. It took a hastily assembled human chain to drag her back to safety.

In the inside back flap of the dust wrapper for *Biggles' Second Case,* there is a telling quote: "Boys like to read something exciting. Don't tell me it's bad for them." (Sydney W. Carroll in the *Daily Sketch*). The same quote is also repeated on the inside flap of the dust wrapper of *Biggles Hunts Big Game.* To me, it indicates that Mildred has not been the first person to voice a criticism against the Biggles books. Mr Carroll's rather defensive stance suggests that he is expecting a backlash of criticism to his seemingly innocent viewpoint.

However, it is not until fifteen years or so after the publication of *Biggles' Second Case*, that Johns and Biggles come under more intense public criticism. During the 1960s and 1970s, hostile criticism from several librarians sees copies of the Biggles books removed from a number of school and public library shelves in both the UK and Australia. Johns finds himself in good company in this respect. At various times, and various places, other children's books, which have found themselves on the banned list of public libraries include *Alice in Wonderland* by Lewis Carroll, *Winnie-the-Pooh* by A. A. Milne, *The Diary of a Young Girl* by Anne Frank and, a personal favourite of mine when I was still in nursery school, *Where the Wild Things Are* by Maurice Sendak. If I ever needed a reason to have my nascent views regarding libraries confirmed, here it was (see *The Seventeen and a Half Pence Paperback*). Sadly, book-banning is once again on the rise in a growing number of predominately Republican states in the US. Suzanne Nossel, chief executive officer of Pen America says: "This censorious movement is… casting a chill over the spirit of open inquiry and intellectual freedom that underpins a flourishing democracy." Mildred: take note.

In Praise of the T-34(76)

For Biggles, the Second World War may have ended but, at an after-school club, in a secondary school on the outskirts of London, in the early 1980s, it was as if the fighting never stopped.

The History curriculum was still dominated by the Second World War, pushing those other conflicts—Roses; Hundred Years; Civil—into an obscure and distant background. As a personal note of achievement, I won the first-year School prize, for my scratch-built—very badly scratch-built—model of a Second World War tank—I can't recall what particular type of tank, and I don't think that it would have been recognisable from the model itself.

The War Gaming Society—it was never really formal enough to deserve the capital letters—involved me and several of my similarly-minded peers setting up and pushing around atop a large landscaped board, a considerable number of Airfix models (see *The Golden Hind and Glue Sniffing*) of tanks, and armoured personnel carriers, and plastic soldiers. In fact, the setting up usually took so long that by the time that all the respective pieces were in their battle positions, it was time to pack them all up again and head off home for tea.

Rather unpatriotically, I found myself admiring the German tanks far more than the British ones. The Panzer V Panther; the all-conquering Panzer VI Tiger; the fast-moving Stug III Assault Gun; the enormous Elefant tank destroyer; maybe no surprise, given that many of these weapons were designed by Ferdinand Porsche. In our club, we were rather *laissez faire* regarding historical accuracy, frequently pitting some of these high-spec. weapons from the later years of the War against patently inferior Matilda II tanks of an earlier vintage.

However, amongst all this heavy armoury, I had one very clear favourite. The Russian T-34(76) tank. And it had to be the '76' model with its 76.2mm gun, not the later T-34(85) with its heavier artillery which, IMHO, sacrificed classic aesthetic good looks for superior combat performance.

The T-34(76) was first produced in 1940. However, it was not until 1941 and the German invasion of the Soviet Union during

Operation Barbarossa, that the tank was deployed in large quantities. The centre of production for the T-34 was the Chelyabinsk Tractor Plant, known as Tankograd, located beyond the Ural mountain range, safe from the German advance. At the time that it came into service, the T-34(76) was superior to any of its contemporaries and even German *Generalfeldmarschall* Ewald von Kleist acknowledged that it was 'the finest tank in the world'. It went on to be the tank produced in the greatest quantities during the Second World War and, even today, there are a number of vehicles still maintained for operational service in the armies of Vietnam, Guinea and Cuba.

My personal love of the tank comes not from its record, or its specifications, but from its appearance. If a tank can be thought of in such terms, I believe that the T-34(76), unlike my scratch-built prize winner, is a design classic.

As well as the goodly number of tanks which remain mobile, a huge number of decommissioned T-34(76)s have found their way into service as monuments or war memorials, or have simply just been abandoned: until very recently, when it was removed for restoration, a T-34—admittedly an 85 variant—nicknamed Strompie has occupied a disused corner of Bermondsey in south London, between Mandela Way and Page's Walk, for the past thirty years. The tank featured in the 1995 film *Richard III* starring Ian McKellen and Annette Bening, and is routinely repainted by local artists; it was painted sky blue in support of the National Health Service during the Covid pandemic.

Fronting the Soviet War Memorial at the Tiergarten in Berlin, two T-34(76)s stand on plinths facing Straße des 17 Juni. I admired the two tanks for a considerable period of time before I noticed that someone was occupying a far superior vantage point than me. Tweeting noisily from the barrel of one of the guns, a small sparrow had established a well-protected home. It was nice to see a once devastating weapon of war ending its days being used for such peaceful ends.

Amongst my own collection of Airfix model tanks, I never possessed a T-34(76). Somehow the plastic reproduction never did justice to the pure grittiness of the sloping steel armour and cast turrets of the original. And it was not long before the War Gaming Society disbanded altogether. I would like to be able to record that its disintegration was because the members discovered more important things in life, like girlfriends, but I can say with some degree of confidence, that none of the members of the War Gaming Society ever had such exotic creatures as girlfriends during those innocent days of secondary school. Instead, it was simply that exams intervened, and mundane matters like revision took precedence and, also, that a new Diplomacy society was formed, which took a lot less time to set up.

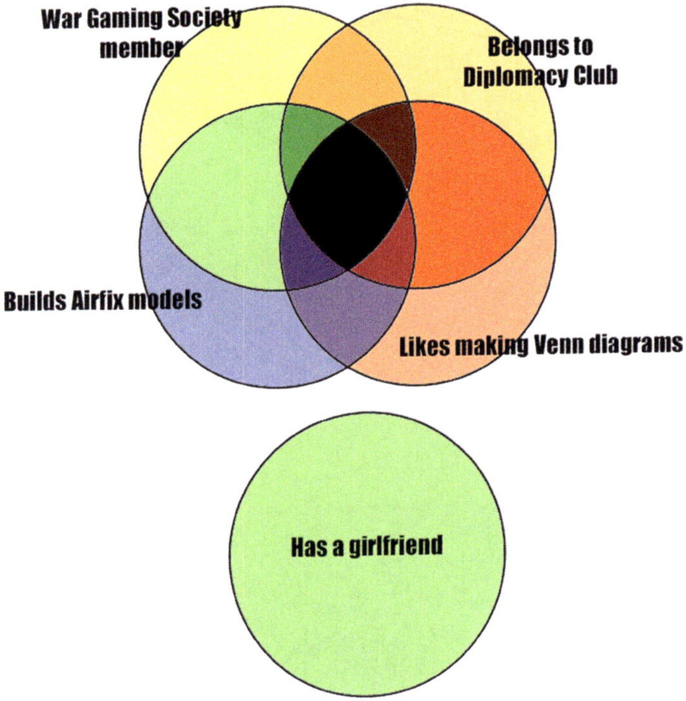
War Gaming Society member
Belongs to Diplomacy Club
Builds Airfix models
Likes making Venn diagrams
Has a girlfriend

The Sunday Afternoon War Movie

In the same way that Saturday afternoon in the 1970s meant Dickie Davies, Giant Haystacks and a medley of televised sport, Sunday afternoon meant sitting down in front of the TV to watch a war movie. The Sunday roast was still being digested; the cold juices were already in the 'fridge congealing nicely for the following day's tea (see *Everything Stops for Tea*); and a soporific calm had descended, which would culminate in my dad falling asleep in front of the TV.

Sometimes the movie was home-grown and a black and white one, which was always a bit depressing: Kenneth More in *Reach for the Sky*; or Richard Todd in *The Dam Busters*; John Mills in *Ice Cold in Alex*; or escape movies *The Colditz Story* or *The Wooden Horse.* Here, the adherence to realism was essential; the story, characters and social message all important. Instead, what I preferred were the big budget Hollywood blockbusters: full technicolour; all action; explosions over conversation.

There were the all-star cast epics like *Battle of the Bulge, Von Ryan's Express* and *A Bridge Too Far*; adaptations of Alistair MacLean stories like *The Guns of Navarone* and *Where Eagles Dare*; and frankly preposterous shoot-'em-ups like *The Dirty Dozen* and *Kelly's Heroes*, which invariably starred someone like Telly Savalas or Clint Eastwood or, sometimes, both.

The store of actors to play Germans in these movies must have been rather limited, and the same few names tended to turn up over and over again: Hardy Krüger; Maximillian Schell; Wolf Kahler. An interesting example of an actor in this category is Anton Diffring. Not necessarily a household name, but an instantly recognisable face, with his blonde hair, pale blue eyes and cold stare, having played a string of Nazis in movies such as *The Heroes of Telemark*, *The Sea Shall Not Have Them*, *Operation Daybreak*, *Escape to Victory*, and was even to be found still typecast playing a Nazi in the Dr Who series *Silver Nemesis*. Ironic that the Nazis should end up providing a career for an actor who was both Jewish and gay.

Reading #16: *Biggles Hunts Big Game*

Is it a contradiction that Biggles can be an action hero one moment and a stamp collector the next? He joins an unlikely band of fellow philatelists: Charlie Chaplin; Franklin D. Roosevelt; Freddie Mercury; even Queen Elizabeth II: "'It may interest you to know that I've always wanted to collect stamps. As a kid at school it was a secret passion with me." (p. 10).

At different stages of my life, I have collected various different things, but never really stamps. This may have been due to having a large stamp collection thrust upon me when I was a boy. While I could admire the variety, colour and decorative design of the different stamps—wonderful dinosaurs from Fujeira; colourful animals from Poland; although the ones from Indonesia were almost uniformly dull, depicting a stern-faced old lad in a *songkok*, whom I can now recognise as President Sukarno; as, similarly, were the ones from Spain, featuring different shades of a balding Franco—there was no enjoyment in acquiring a collection fully-formed. A vital part of any collection is the amassing of it and, the more tortuous and difficult this task is to do, the more enjoyment that the collection ultimately brings. For me, the 'hunt' is as important as the final assembly of items. There is something primeval about the activity, awakening latent hunter-gatherer instincts, which have lain dormant since the time when my ancient ancestors hunted woolly mammoths across the wide plains of Europe.

Biggles own hunt might be initiated by stamps but, as the title of the book suggests, his goal is bigger game; thankfully, not the wildlife of Central Africa where the book is set, but the international criminals gangs, which he identifies are a new kind of criminal: "'Men with brains and capital to back their projects. They do not think in pounds or even hundreds of pounds. They start with thousands and their goal is millions.'" (p. 16).

In describing this new kind of criminal, for whom borders are no longer an obstacle, W. E. Johns is unwittingly describing a new world order, which will be the dominant economic driver for the remainder of the 20th century, and the start of the next: globalisation. Where Biggles talks about flying crooks—"...he can get anywhere in the world in a few hours. There are no frontiers in the sky, no barricades, nothing to stop him... He can make his headquarters where he likes, and from there strike in any direction." (p. 18)—he could just as easily be describing the modern-day multinational corporation.

The location of Kudinga in *Biggles Hunts Big Game* corresponds fairly accurately to the Bengangai Game Reserve in current-day South Sudan. The Central Africa setting of the book is interesting: Biggles describes the location of the hunting lodge, which is the centre of the story, as being located: "...at the point where the territories of the Anglo-Egyptian Sudan, French Equatorial Africa and the Belgian Congo, touch." (p. 49). It is a graphic example of the way that Africa was colonised and divided up between the European powers at the time. Anglo-Egyptian Sudan corresponds to territory, which is now divided between Sudan and South Sudan; French Equatorial Africa was a large region, which now comprises the countries of the Central African Republic, the Republic of Congo, Chad, and Gabon; whilst Belgian Congo is now the Democratic Republic of the Congo. The fallout of the Scramble for Africa, which left almost ninety percent of Africa under European control by the start of the First World War was still very much the status quo, and it was not until ten years after the time that Johns was writing *Biggles Hunts Big Game* that the process of the decolonisation of Africa began, with Ghana—formerly the Gold Coast—gaining independence from Britain in 1957.

The Nascent Collector

At the time that I was a member of the War Gaming Society at school (see *In Praise of the T-34(76)*), I had assembled a considerable number of Airfix model airplanes, ships and tanks, but were they a collection? On some levels, they might be thought so. I used to display them with the same kind of pride as that of a collector; I acquired them periodically over a long period, as and when my pocket money would permit; and there was a consistency of theme running throughout all the items. But there was something missing. A vital ingredient, which meant that I never really thought about them as a collection. It was the *intent* behind why I was buying these items in the first place. It was the same with all my Action Man gear (see *Action Man: Deep Sea Diver*); whilst the ends might appear to lead to a collection, the means suggested something else. Neither the models nor the Action Men were gathered with the *aim* in mind of forming a collection. I was simply acquiring them for the purposes of play: the models to make up and then use in my strategy games; the Action Men to dress up and stage play fights between each other in the back garden. My sea life, though. That was an entirely different kettle of… well, fish, altogether. That was a collection.

I must have started with a few fossils, partially inspired by Mary Anning (see *Mary Anning and Joan Worralson*). My Auntie Edie's back garden in Leigh-on-Sea was laid with pebbles, and I would spend many fruitless hours scouring through them in the hope of finding the fossilised imprint of a sea urchin, or the distinctive spirals of an ammonite. My family would sometimes take summer holidays to either the Kent or the Dorset coast, and I used to delight in looking through the contents of the little shops by the sea front, which had baskets outside full of cowrie shells and spiky conches, and window displays crammed with more exotic-looking spiral shells from distant seas, dried starfish, and large fossils, looking like they were still trying to escape from the black rock, which encased them. Sometimes, if I had any money left over after having spent it on all the requisite plastic goods necessary for an English beach holiday—bucket, spade, ball—I would buy something from one of these shops, and add them to the stones, which I had squirreled away from Auntie Edie's back garden. And in this way the collection grew. On one seaside trip, I discovered washed up on the shore a strange soft yellow ball, which I thought must be a sea sponge, and which I thought that I could dry and add to my collection. I hid the object away in the back of my dad's car, where it proceeded to simply rot, emitting such a ghastly fishy smell that it stank out the car for the entire journey home. Rather than a sea sponge, it turned out to be a bundle of empty egg cases of the common whelk. Needless to say, it was binned as soon as we got home.

I cannot recall at what point I decided to display my collection, but it must have been fairly early on. Rather than drag out the small, cardboard box, which had provided their erstwhile home, every time that I wanted to show someone my latest exhibit, instead I cleared a small space on top of the bookshelf in my bedroom, and began the task of arranging and curating. My most prized possessions were a dried puffer fish, complete with spiky quills and surprised Botex-lips pursed mouth, and a stuffed piranha, which could have been a trophy obtained from the taxidermists featured in *Biggles Hunts Big Game*.

Why sea life for a collection? Why indeed. Why anything for that matter? There is an altogether bigger question there, lurking in the background. It all comes back to that question from Mr Clayton's first year geography class (see *The Best Things in Life are Free*). What is the meaning of (sea)life?

The end of my sea life collection began with the discovery of a blackbird's skull in my back garden. It was a perfect little skull, delicate and intricate; a talking point, ready for display. However, it had nothing to do with sea life. It was a cuckoo amongst the shells and the crab carapaces and the stuffed fish. With its inclusion, my collection began to lose its integrity. From that moment, its demise was inevitable.

I cannot recall what happened to the collection in the end. It must have been returned to a, slightly larger, cardboard box; stored away to gradually gather dust, until such time that it was sufficiently forgotten that my parents could consign it to the same fate as the malodorous whelk egg cases.

The Decolonisation of Education

Decolonisation in the 21st century has moved beyond the physical withdrawal of personnel and the instruments and regulations of state power by the invaders of a colonised territory. Recent years have seen a move towards the decolonisation of education, such that the canon of established texts is revised and reappraised through a non-colonial lens, and indigenous knowledge is given greater weighting.

The decolonisation of education allows for a re-examination of the shared assumptions and unconscious biases that everyone has about different cultures and areas of the world. It examines questions about the subject and the identity of the writer. Ultimately, knowledge is a far more important battleground than any territory and, in the modern world, it is assailed on all sides by 'fake news', race-to-the-bottom social media pedalled ignorance, and politically and commercially motivated lies. The battle for possession of the narrative has never been more important or more fiercely contested.

Without challenging received wisdom we do not progress and move towards a global society and a diverse world view; at the same time, it is important that the sources from which we derive our information are trustworthy, peer-reviewed and authentic.

During the years that W. E. Johns was writing he would have witnessed a huge change in his world—culturally, politically, geographically. Despite being a product of the colonial period, his outlook was much more modern; he was not someone who was wedded to the past, and he reflected the changes that he witnessed occurring around him in his writing.

The decolonisation of education has sometimes—wrongly—been described as taking the curriculum back from 'dead white men'. Dead white men like Johns. This is not the case. It is about opening minds to all viewpoints. Asking questions. As I have said before (see *The Crystal Skull*), we don't know how much we know until we know how little we know, and the goal of decolonising education should be to get people asking more questions, so that we add to the sum total of human knowledge, not to narrow it.

Reading #17: *Biggles Follows On*

For the entire duration of Biggles' career working as a detective in the Special Air Police, the prevailing political backdrop was that of the Cold War. The term describes the state of geopolitical suspicion, which existed between the United States and the Soviet Union, and their respective allies, roughly from the end of the Second World War to the fall of the Berlin Wall in 1989, the collapse of Communist rule in eastern Europe, and the subsequent break-up of the Soviet Union itself in 1991. So, it was perhaps inevitable that Biggles would find himself mixed up in several cases, which he would ultimately discover contained a political angle to them.

Biggles himself is shown not to have a particularly high opinion of communism as an ideology: "'I have yet to meet a Communist who wasn't interested in money. It's not having any that makes him a Communist.'" (p. 71). The Berlin that Biggles visits in *Biggles Follows On* (Hodder, 1952) is a very different city to the modern-day capital of Germany. At the time, the city was divided into three zones, one controlled by Britain, another by the US, and the third by the Soviet Union. The actual Berlin Wall was not constructed until 1961, but the concept of an 'Iron Curtain' dividing the western and eastern halves of Berlin was very much in place: "You might get behind the Iron Curtain by dropping in by an aircraft; but I can't see you getting out again." (p. 43). The book was written bang in the middle of the Korean War. The War saw the Soviet-backed Democratic People's Republic of Korea in conflict with the US-backed Republic of Korea, and escalated from a civil conflict to a proxy war between clashing superpowers, with the backdrop a battle between communism and democracy.

Undercover in Berlin, allows Biggles to display his extensive knowledge of foreign languages: "...he automatically answered '*Ja*'." (pp 51-52). Throughout his career, Biggles is revealed to be a genuine polyglot, fluent in French, German and Hindi—having been born and raised in India—and picking up Norwegian with incredible alacrity during a wartime assignment there: "To live in a country is the best and quickest way of learning its language, and after seven weeks of concentrated effort Biggles was able to carry on a normal conversation in Norwegian." (*Biggles Defies the Swastika*, p. 13). To my discredit, I have never shared with Biggles this same ability. I have never made that transition of finding myself *thinking* in a different language; forever ponderously translating back and forth; often ending up speaking a jumbled hotchpotch of several different languages, and rarely the correct one at the correct time.

The book also sees a head-on collision between two of W. E. Johns' different series. Although Biggles has occasionally appeared as a very minor character in some of the Gimlet stories, and the book *Comrades in Arms* (Hodder, 1947) features separate stories about Biggles, Gimlet and Worrals, *Biggles Follows On* is the first—and only—occasion when Captain Lorrington King, known to all as 'Gimlet' and his team of commandos—'Copper' Coulson,

'Trapper' Troublay and 'Cub' Peters—feature so prominently in a Biggles series book. It is a successful marrying of the two strands of Johns' writing, although Gimlet and Bertie's bantering about fox-hunting and racehorses seems slightly contrived: "'I remember, out huntin', how she watched for the rabbit holes.'" (p. 155). The back cover of the dust wrapper for *Biggles Follows On* contains a long, promotional letter, ostensibly written by Johns' introducing the Gimlet books to the Biggles audience, with a warning that "His methods are not always as gentlemanly as Biggles."

I find it amusing that the name of the Guardsman that Biggles and Gimlet endeavour to rescue from behind the Iron Curtain is Ross. I wonder if this is a case of Johns gaining a bit of tongue-in-cheek comeuppance on T. E. Lawrence after their less-than-successful encounter in 1922 (see *Reading #3: Biggles Flies East*); a case of revenge best served cold. Johns describes Ross as "…a tall, fair, good-looking lad… his blue eyes stared straight ahead." (p. 24). Whilst the blue eyes and fair hair might describe T. E. Lawrence, the man himself was relatively short, standing five feet and five inches.

The story also provided a reminder of another list from childhood (see *The Naming of Parts*): international vehicle registration codes. For me, these codes took the form of car's registration plates; for Biggles, it was aircraft: "They moved on towards the aircraft bearing the OK registration letters of Czechoslovakia." (p. 55). I was always interested in the registration letters, which did not match up precisely alphabetically with the country they belonged to. At the time, I had not realised that the 'D' for Germany meant 'Deutschland'; it was simply a puzzle why the letter used was not a 'G'. Similarly, 'CH' for Switzerland was an inexplicable enigma, not knowing that it represented 'Confœdoratio Helvetica'. Urban legend has it that the 'OK' for Czechoslovakia came about because the Czech delegation assigned to decide the matter of their country's registration code did not speak much English, and when asked for their choice simply replied in good-natured and uncomprehending agreement: "Okay." Like *Biggles Follows On*, it makes for a good story.

The Psychology of Collecting

A lot has been written about the psychology of collecting and, from listening to all the experts, it would be easy to conclude that a propensity towards collecting ranks right up there with some of the most deviant behaviour known to mankind.

Sigmund Freud linked collecting with unresolved toilet training issues; revealing, for a man who amassed a vast collection of art and antiques himself. Other psychologists suggest that collecting is an attempt to impose a small area of order in a world of chaos. It has been suggested that a collection is the physical manifestation of a person's inner life, and through that collection it is possible to diagnose that individual's various ills—psychological, political, social. Why ills? Why not positive attributes?

People collect for many reasons. As I have mentioned before (see *Reading #16: Biggles Hunts Big Game*), for me a large element of collecting is the thrill of the hunt; the means is often more important than the ends. Other motivations for collecting have been identified as: to gain knowledge; in appreciation of beauty; to gain pride in ownership; the competitive challenge; for financial gain; to meet with fellow enthusiasts; from nostalgia; pure altruism; to archive and preserve; to achieve status and recognition; as a sign of affiliation; as relaxation; and for pure pleasure. Most of these reasons, I would consider as being fairly innocent; pretty positive.

Of course, collecting—like so many other things—has the potential to become compulsive, and there lies a darker world, a fictional example of which was chillingly and evocatively described in P. M. Hubbard's excellent novel *A Hive of Glass* (Michael Joseph, 1965).

Is it possible to self-analyse when your own collecting has crossed over to the dark side? Quite possibly not. In my case, I could always ask my wife what she thinks about my collection but, then again, she collects even more stuff than I do, so she is probably not best placed to offer an objective opinion.

Reading #18: *Biggles in the Blue*

It is a slightly scary sensation for a middle-aged man to suddenly wake up one day with the realisation that all the elements of himself that he believed defined his own peculiar individuality and which were entirely unique to him are actually nothing more than the influences of a third party. I experienced that feeling when re-reading *Biggles in the Blue.*

Biggles in the Blue had always been one of my favourite of the Biggles stories since childhood but, if asked, I would have been hard-pressed to give an explanation precisely why this was the case. Reading the book as an adult, I can find within the book all the various strands of interests, which have followed me throughout my lifetime: there is the focus on islands—on this occasion Biggles is sent to Jamaica and the Bahamas archipelago—"…all islands, coral islands, desert islands or treasure islands, sandy, palm-clad or rocky, hold a fascination of their own." (p. 76); there is a theme of ornithology—in this instance, a colony of rare flamingos; there is much about collecting: "Evans, like most enthusiastic collectors, was only too willing to talk about the subject nearest his heart." (p. 55); could this even be the inspiration for the mysterious sea-life collection? (see *The Nascent Collector*): "On the mantelpiece, flanking a brass-faced clock, was an assortment of sea shells." (p. 49). It is all here; all the little elements that fit together and make up me, all contained in one slender, 192-page book. Bradley Dunbar as created by W. E. Johns. No small wonder that the book is one of my favourites; it is like having a conversation with oneself; like looking at a familiar reflection in the mirror.

At the same time that W. E. Johns was writing *Biggles in the Blue*, another writer was attempting to write his first novel: Ian Fleming. There are interesting parallels between the two books. The location for much of the action in *Biggles in the Blue* is Jamaica, and it was on Jamaica, in the early months of 1952, that Ian Fleming began writing *Casino Royale*, the first novel to feature secret agent, 007, James Bond. Fleming first visited Jamaica during a wartime summit in 1942, and had his house *Goldeneye* built there in 1945, a property he would regularly visit for long periods each winter. *Casino Royale* was published by Jonathan Cape in April 1953, one month after the first part of *Biggles in the Blue* was published in *The Eagle* comic; the book itself being published by Brockhampton Press in July of the same year.

Fleming stated that he borrowed Bond's name from the American ornithologist James Bond who was an expert on birds of the Caribbean and author of the book *Field Guide of Birds of the West Indies: A Guide to All the Species of Birds Known from the Greater Antilles, Lesser Antilles and Bahama Islands* (Macmillan, 1947). The fictional Bond himself is described as a commander in the Royal Naval Reserve. In *Biggles in the Blue*, one of the first people that Biggles interviews is a retired British naval commander named Evans, whose chief interest in life is natural history and who "…is writing a book on the birds of the West Indies." (p. 23).

Fleming's sixth novel, *Dr No* (Jonathan Cape, 1958) was also written at *Goldeneye.* In this book, a large part of the action actually takes place in the Caribbean, with Dr Julius No's hideout being the fictional island of Crab Key. Unlike the popular image of a Caribbean island of golden sands, swaying palm trees and clear, turquoise seas, Crab Key is a harsh, unforgiving landscape of marshland and swamp, one end of which is home to a large colony of roseate spoonbills. Sound familiar? In *Biggles in the Blue*, Johns describes the island of Great Inagua, the second largest island in the Bahamas group as "…sheer desolation… tufts of coarse grey grass growing between the caked mud of what had obviously been puddles of stagnant water." (p. 106), inhabited by "…innumerable land crabs, large yellow creatures with eyes set on stalks and mouths that opened sideways to give their faces a demoniac expression." (p. 107). In the book—and in real life, too—the island is home to a large colony of American flamingos. Johns based his colony of flamingos on the end of the island furthest away from the main settlement at Matthew Town, whereas today the birds occupy the salt flats around Lake Rosa. At the time that Johns was writing, the flamingos on Inagua were in danger of extinction, their numbers down to just a few thousand birds, not because of humans stealing their eggs as Johns suggests: "Mathew Town would have raided the nesting ground and wiped out the whole colony." (p. 162), but because wild pigs, introduced by early settlers were destroying the eggs and the young birds. However, thanks to many decades of conservation efforts, the flamingos on Inagua now number more than 80,000 birds.

An observant ornithologist will probably recognise that the flamingos in my own photograph are not the bright scarlet American flamingos, which live on Inagua, but the Greater flamingo. This is because the photograph was taken not in the Caribbean, but at Saintes-Maries-de-la-Mer in the Camargue in the south of France. One thing that I did share with Biggles on Inagua, though, was that I got bitten to pieces by mosquitoes taking the photograph at sunset.

Did Ian Fleming read Biggles? It seems quite likely. One man who would surely have known is John Pearson. Pearson was Fleming's assistant at the *Sunday Times* and wrote biographies of Fleming, Bond, and Biggles, too—*The Life of Ian Fleming* (Jonathan

Cape, 1966); *James Bond: The Authorized Biography of 007* (Sidgwick and Jackson, 1973); and *Biggles: The Authorised Biography* (Sidgwick and Jackson, 1978). However, under the pseudonym Henry Cloud he also wrote a biography of Barbara Cartland—*Barbara Cartland: Crusader in Pink* (Weidenfeld and Nicholson, 1979)—someone who I would imagine is slightly less likely to have read Biggles, so perhaps there is not too much inference that can be drawn there. Is it too fanciful to suggest that, perhaps like me, Fleming discovered in *Biggles in the Blue* a convergence of multiple strands of his own personality, which he later went on to use in his own writing?

I don't think that Mildred would have approved of Ian Fleming any more than she did Biggles, and the entire James Bond oeuvre would have simply been more fuel for her bonfire. She might also have taken exception to an instance of attributing national characteristics in *Biggles in the Blue*: "'That fellow over there,' he indicated the original object of their visit, 'is a Slav from Eastern Europe, judging from his flat face and high cheekbones.'" (p. 45). Biggles is in good company here, though. Hollywood has been resorting to national stereotypes for its villains for decades. During and immediately after the Second World War, the Germans and Japanese obviously provided an easy source of evil-doers for the big screen; before that, in the Thirties, it had been the Chinese, and later, in the midst of the Cold War, the Russians. Then, towards the end of the 1980s, for an all-too brief period, a strange thing happened. It was as if there were suddenly no wars; no obvious bad guys. A new villain was needed, and so up stepped the evil Brit. Jeremy Irons was given a career-makeover from *Brideshead* to *Die Hard*. However, it was not long before Saddam Hussein began posturing in the Middle East, and a new breed of Arab villains was conceived, a situation only exacerbated after 9/11. And, so, what next for Hollywood? Sadly, there is little need to exert too much imagination. We are back to the future. Hello, Russia, my old friend.

The Start of My Biggles Collection

When did my Biggles books start to become a collection? Not when I was a boy, I think. Back then, the books were purely functional. They accumulated because I was reading them, in the same way that socks accumulated because I was wearing them. And, as with so many items for which no special sentimental attachment has been invested, they were cast aside with glib abandon. Looking back, over the years, certain Biggles titles I must have bought and then discarded, only to repurchase again, as frequently as a snake sheds its skin. That formative experience in Arundel (see *A Disappointment in Arundel*) must have given my younger self an inkling that there was a monetary value attached to certain of the Biggles books and, I cannot deny that some of the books I have acquired I have sold myself for a modest profit—twice I have had pass through my grubby, commercial fingers first edition copies of *Biggles Flies East*, complete with the rare original dust wrapper and, on both occasions I sold them; so, it is entirely my own fault that the copy of *Biggles Flies East* that I currently own has only a facsimile wrapper. This might suggest that I had fulfilled one of the possible criteria for collecting: collecting for financial gain (see *The Psychology of Collecting*). But I would disagree. Then I was *acquiring* for financial gain, not collecting. For me, my true Biggles collection began when I *stopped* acquiring for financial gain, and my focus shifted to seeing the books as objects above and beyond the function of purely reading them.

I was no longer satisfied with a cheap paperback; no longer prepared to try to retype the entire text of a borrowed library copy of *Biggles Investigates*—I got to page 9 for anyone who is interested; I desired to hunt out first edition hardbacks. In the big game hunting world of book collecting, these were the 'Big Five'; the lions, leopards, rhinos, elephants and buffalo. But, in the same way that Hilary Mantel wrote about her husband's Biggles collection: "My husband has 85 of these titles, and rules about his collection. He has to happen upon the books, not hunt them down. He won't pay silly money, and he'll have nothing to do with catalogues, internet searches or specialist networks." (*The Guardian*, 12 December 2009), I, too, impose certain rules on the books I amass, and this has led to certain strange anomalies. For instance, I do not currently have in my collection a copy of *Biggles and the Pirate Treasure* (Brockhampton Press, 1954), which is a relatively easy title to acquire, and where there are currently dozens of copies available for sale on the internet. Why? Because, subconsciously, I have set myself a limit to the amount of money that I am prepared to pay for this particular book, and it is a relatively low amount, something in the region of £20, give or take a pound or two. Now, I also know that there is currently a copy advertised on eBay for less than this amount. So, why don't I snap it up? Because the dust wrapper has a lot of green gunk on the front, and I want to find a nicer copy than that. So, my collection has a few basic, but unspoken, rules. The book must seem like 'value for money'—regardless of just how much money that criteria might equate to–—and no green gunk on the cover.

Of course, when it comes to amassing a collection of books—a collection of anything, really—the advent of the internet changed everything. Almost overnight the ranks of second-hand bookshops, which used to line each side of Charing Cross Road began to close and disappear; the places where it was possible to physically rummage became fewer. At the same time, the entire world was suddenly searchable at the flick of a computer keystroke. Books that had previously been virtually unobtainable instantly fell into one of three clearly defined categories: books that are easily obtainable; books that are easily obtainable but very expensive; books that are still virtually unobtainable, no matter how much love or money. Into the first category would be something like a first edition of *Biggles and the Pirate's Treasure.* Into the second category might be a copy of *Biggles and the Deep Blue Sea* (Brockhampton Press, 1968) or *Biggles Does Some Homework* (Norman Wright, 1998); and into the last category might be a nice first edition of *The Camels are Coming* in original dust wrapper.

Another rule regarding my collection is that it must grow organically. What I mean by this rather pretentious statement is that I wish to build it up in dribs and drabs; I have no desire to inherit someone else's collection fully formed. Collecting is a process. How much easier it would have been to simply have stuck to reading.

Did Someone Mention Ornithology?

I have always loved Nature; it is growing older that the love has coalesced more around birds. Probably because they are more omnipresent in my life than many other forms of wildlife. I can look out into my back garden and see birds every single day, whereas other creatures take a little more hunting out, even the annoying rat, who regularly nibbles behind my skirting boards. I make no claims to being a twitcher; I openly admit that I struggle to tell one of Bill Oddie's 'little brown birds' from another; I simply enjoy attempting to spot and identify whatever species of bird happens to fly across my path. That is not to say that I haven't occasionally been possessed by the odd obsession. For a long time, it was puffins. They took me to Lundy, where I saw just one, a distant speck on a grey sea, which I could scarcely recognise even through the warden's powerful binoculars; they took me to remote and rocky Bleiksøya in the north of Norway, where the lowering mist defeated my objective; and to the island of Værøy in the Lofotens, where I arrived after the puffin season had ended. Finally, I caught up with my quarry on a wet and windy walk along the Gobbins Cliff Path in Northern Ireland, where I was able to watch the beautiful birds emerge from their burrows, stretch their little wings, and fly out towards the Irish Sea. My puffin obsession was satisfied. But no sooner has one obsession ended and a new one rears its ugly head. Now, I fear, it is ospreys.

It is easy to discuss bird watching in the same kind of terms as that used to describe collecting. For twitchers, this is very much the case: the compilation and ticking off of species sighted; the active pursuit of rare species; the community of fellow enthusiasts. In November 2021, I was staying at the Windmill at Cley-next-the-Sea in Norfolk, alternately hunkering down to avoid the worst of Storm Arwen and venturing out to explore the marshes and tidal flats, when I encountered a gathering of twitchers taking refuge in a drab, brick shelter on the shingle, their long camera lenses all trained in the same direction out to sea.

"What are you looking at?" I asked.

"Brünnich's Guillemot," one replied.

Sadly, two days later, the object of their scrutiny, was washed up dead on a sandbank at Wells-next-the-Sea.

In *Biggles in the Blue*, Ginger admits to once having pursued the rather dubious hobby of collecting bird's eggs: "'When I was a kid I used to collect eggs myself,' he confessed." (*Biggles in the Blue*, p. 51), and even Commander Evans admits to having his eye on possessing a rare flamingo egg: "'I shouldn't really tell you this because it's almost a confession of law-breaking.'" (*Biggles in the Blue*, p. 55).

As with most things in life, it is easier to see the faults in, and be critical of, someone else's behaviour than it is to objectively analyse one's own.

Reading #19: *Biggles and the Leopards of Zinn*

They say never judge a book by its cover but, sometimes, you've got to judge a book by its title and, judging by its title, *Biggles and the Leopards of Zinn* is an absolute cracker. And the front cover of the first edition, published by Brockhampton Press in 1960, is none too shabby either. I never owned a copy of *Biggles and the Leopards of Zinn* when I was a boy; it was one of the titles that I frequently saw listed in the bibliography, which was published either in the front, or the back of the dust wrapper, of many of the Biggles books, and it became the book that I most wished to read, simply because the title was so evocative. Mysterious. What, who or where was Zinn? Why were there leopards there? What was Biggles' involvement with them? The title never appeared in Old Mr Carr's shop (see *Old Pence and Cat's Piss*); it was never reissued as a popular paperback; I could find no trace of it in all my local haunts. Its obscurity and elusiveness rendered it all the more desirable.

Boyhood passed and I never did get to read a copy of *Biggles and the Leopards of Zinn.* In early adulthood, I did *see* a copy at an antiquarian book fair in London's Royal National Hotel, but these were my 'wilderness years' in terms of reading Biggles and, although I did register a certain interest in finally discovering what was the picture on the front of the dust wrapper, my mind was on other matters, like finding a job, and a home, and a girlfriend, and

I let the copy slip through my fingers. It was only later that I finally purchased a copy for myself, from a bookshop on the internet, but I can still recall the excitement waiting for the copy to arrive in the post. And when it did arrive? Well, the title was still a cracker, and the front cover was still none too shabby, but the story…? In the end, I found it a little disappointing. Perhaps my expectations had just been too great? I had invested too much anticipation into a single book, and it was impossible for the reality to live up to the dream.

And yet, it is still an exciting story, filled with numerous perils from both wild creatures and dangerous ne'er-do-wells but, for some reason, I find the tone of the book slightly depressing; unusual for a W. E. Johns' story. In part, I think this is because of the writing style of the book: in one or two places, Johns interjects an external author's voice to over-explain certain elements of the book, and I find this slightly clunky: "It will now be understood why he had flown to the seldom-visited Lake Jumu, what he hoped to achieve, and why he was taking precautions more elaborate than usual." (p. 37). It is also necessary to review the book against the backdrop of world events at the time of publication. In *Biggles and the Leopards of Zinn*, Johns returns Biggles to territory that he has previously explored in *Biggles in Africa* (Oxford, 1936), *Biggles Hunts Big Game* and *Biggles and the Black Raider* (Hodder, 1953). This is the centre of Africa; a point at the convergence of several countries; metaphorically, if not *quite* geographically, at Joseph Conrad's *Heart of Darkness*; a place perceived to be beyond the reach of Law, where African and European alike can act with impunity. However, as Prime Minister Harold Macmillan said in his famous 'Wind of Change' speech in February 1960, the sentiments of which Bob Dylan neatly paraphrased in the title of his album of 1964, 'The Times They Are a-Changin''. More and more British territories in Africa were gaining independence, some through mutual agreement—Nigeria became an independent state in October 1960—some only after many years of civil unrest and bloody conflict—the Kenya Land and Freedom Army, or *Mau Mau*, fought a war against the British authorities for eight years from 1952 to 1960; Kenya eventually gaining its independence in December 1963. Biggles comments on the state of affairs: "'…someone is deliberately trying to unsettle the Zinns and so cause trouble. The same sort of thing is going on all over Africa.'"

(p. 85). There is a sense that Johns is resigned to the changes that are occurring, not just in Africa but all around the world with Britain's loss of Empire, and yet he still remains to be entirely convinced that it is a change for the better and, for me, in *Biggles and the Leopards of Zinn*, I feel Johns' conflicted emotions and scepticism in his written words. There is a subtle change in some of Johns' language, too; not sufficiently subtle to prevent Mildred from adding the book to her teetering pyre but, nevertheless, something that I find interesting. Where an instance of the N-word still appears in *Biggles and the Leopards of Zinn* (p. 78), it is not voiced by either Biggles or any of his compatriots, but by one of the baddies of the piece, indicating a shift of use from casual description to recognised insult. Similarly, Biggles talks about "a monkey in the woodpile' (p. 39), where in a previous time, his language might have been more graphic. However, any positive shift is rather undone by Bertie's persistent joke about one of the local tribesmen: "'We like him. We're keeping him for a house-pet.'" (p. 78), and there is still a tone of patronising colonialism and romantic idealism in Biggles' albeit well-intentioned conclusion to leave the Zinns to live "in a little world of their own, far from the scares of hydrogen bombs and other horrors civilisation is producing." (p. 183).

Although *Biggles and the Leopards of Zinn* is not one of my favourite books in the series, it did provide me with the answer to one of my earlier questions: what, who, or where was Zinn? The Zinns turned out to be an imaginary tribe, living on the shores of the imaginary Lake Jubu, where they eke out a meagre existence catching fish from the lake. This put me in mind of an anecdote that Colonel Stok recounts in Len Deighton's third spy novel *Funeral in Berlin* (Jonathan Cape, 1964): "There is a village in Africa where the tribesmen stand in the deep crocodile-infested water, fishing. They send the fish they catch for barter to the next village where the main industry is manufacturing wooden legs… That's capitalism."

Biggles' Top Tips

'Biggles Saved My Life'. It was the headline of many newspapers and news sites on Thursday 13 August 2009. The previous day, pilot Vince Hagedorn had crashed his light aircraft into a tree on a golf course on the outskirts of Dundee. He attributed the fact that he managed to survive to having read a story of Biggles trying to land a plane after its engine had been shot up over enemy lines: "He tries to get back to the airfield and doesn't quite make it and ends up with no height over a wood. As he flies into the wood, he pulls the stick back to pancake into the trees. And I did just that. I just stalled into the trees." (BBC News Channel, 13 August 2009).

A 'pancake' landing—technically an emergency landing in which an aircraft levels out close to the ground and drops vertically with its engine off and undercarriage retracted— is nothing new to Biggles, but the story, which most closely resembles the circumstances of Vince Hagedorn's crash, is *Biggles Goes Ballooning*, first published in *The Modern Boy* magazine in July 1934; subsequently as *Down to Earth* and *A Desperate Chance* in *Biggles in France* (Amalgamated Press, 1935), and then as *A Ride to Remember* in *Biggles of 266* (Thames Publishing Co., 1956).

The Biggles books actually provide a wealth of useful tips, not just for amateur pilots, but for people in all walks of life and in many different circumstances. Antipodean Biggles collector, Tony Wiles, describes how he put to practical use some Biggles-wisdom during a long cross-country car journey: "I was driving from Sydney to Perth (over 4000kms) in 1989 and nearing the South Australian/West Australian border, my fuel pump started to leak. Having read Biggles and his using chewing gum to patch up leaks, I decided to try this. It worked and I got to Kalgoolie using this method. No fuel pump was available in Kalgoolie, so I continued on to Perth using the same method. Safe to say, I arrived."

In *Biggles in Africa*, Biggles has a tip for the plane-less and the car-less but who is required to walk a long distance: "He sat down and proceeded to take off his shoes and change the socks from one foot to the other. 'It's an old army dodge,' he said." (*Biggles in Africa*, p. 176).

In *Biggles and the Leopards of Zinn*, Biggles describes a method for purifying water, which I thought that I could try out at home: "Biggles made a simple but practical filter, to remove solids from the water, by burning black some slices of bread. Through this all water for drinking would be passed before being boiled." (*Biggles and the Leopards of Zinn*, p. 38).

I'm not quite sure that I would risk drinking the resultant liquid, but it succeeded in turning a very muddy glass of water into a slightly less muddy glass of water. Made a horrible soggy mess of a decent bit of toast, though.

Reading #20: *Biggles Scores a Bull*

Which young schoolboy doesn't want to know all about the finer intricacies of cattle stock breeding techniques? W. E. Johns certainly knows how to give his audience what they want! These sentiments found an echo in the comments of a strangely anonymous teacher from a similarly anonymous school on the inside back flap to the dust wrapper of *Biggles Hunts Big Game*: "Boys will find in these books all the thrills and excitement they seek for in their reading." (quote attributed to 'English master of a Secondary Modern School').

I have always been a greater reader of fiction than I have of non-fiction, but I also find that fiction is a great source of factual information and, often, on subjects that I would never dream to find out about otherwise. Cattle breeding being a case in point. I am extremely unlikely to ever want to read an entire non-fiction book about cattle breeding, but to be presented with a test-tube sized amount via the pages of fiction is an opportunity to increase my knowledge, which I am not going to turn down. Johns is a master at interweaving nuggets of fact into an exciting fictional storyline; learning by osmosis. I have often wondered how I have picked up certain pieces of general knowledge that I possess; certain facts I know; phrases I understand, but, in many cases, I need look no further than the pages of a Biggles book to discover the origin of this learning. Is there a similar source for children growing up today? Do the Harry Potter books of J. K. Rowling provide a similarly rich fact-based education? Maybe it doesn't matter. I think the nature of handling knowledge has changed during the past generation. With the advent of the internet, there is not such an imperative to store up a resource of *personal* general knowledge; perhaps more important is the ability to know how to swiftly access the shared pool of knowledge. The danger then is to be able to assess the veracity of that knowledge. When learning, you need to be able to trust your source. At school, it is to be hoped that the teacher is a reliable source of information; on the internet, it is much more of a minefield. For me, I was confident in my childhood guide: in W. E. Johns I trust.

I suspect Johns of having a little fun in the writing of *Biggles Scores a Bull*. As well as the obvious pun in the title—for a book, which involves Biggles investigating a gang of cattle rustlers—he also smatters the text with several well-known colloquialisms, all of which have a farmyard connection: "'Hold your horses,' said Ginger." (p. 35); "'There used to be a joke about flying pigs but there's nothing funny about that now.'" (p. 13); "'…it must have gone as meek as a lamb.'" (pp 26-27).

In contrast to this humour, though, Johns also deals with some fairly sober subjects: in *Biggles Scores a Bull*, a case of suicide. It is something else for which Johns was subjected to criticism in his writing career: that some of his descriptions and subjects were too 'grown-up' to be read by young school children. Certainly, he never shied away from graphic descriptions, but this is what made the stories the more believable, and exciting, and authentic. Children can be the sternest critics when they spot anything that strikes them as being patronising or that does not ring true, and Johns treated his junior audience with the respect they deserved, and did not attempt to sentimentalise or whitewash some of the horrors that he recounts, whether it is death, injury, or even drug addiction. In *Biggles Scores a Bull*, the doctor's pronouncement of the suicide is as matter of fact as Michael Caine's similarly worded statement when the van blows up in *The Italian Job*: "'There's nothing I can do, nothing anyone can do,' he stated simply. 'He's blown half his head off.'" (p. 156). Similarly, in *Biggles – Air Commodore* (Oxford University Press, 1937), Johns does not mince his words when describing how Biggles rescues a sailor from a shark-infested sea: "'Great heaven! Where's all this blood coming from?' he cried in a horror-stricken voice. Then he saw, and shuddered. The unfortunate sailor's right foot had been bitten clean off above the ankle." (*Biggles – Air Commodore*, p. 60). And, in *Another Job for Biggles* (Hodder, 1951), he describes the paranoia of a drug trip: "Then he became two people, one in the throes of delirium and the other watching. An icy chill began to creep through his limbs." (*Another Job for Biggles,* p. 108).

I experienced my own instance of an icy chill creeping through my limbs when I read another, seemingly very innocent passage in *Biggles Scores a Bull*: "'He tells me he's a scout.'" (p. 35). I was never a Scout when I was at school. Neither was I a Cub. Here's the thing. At the age of seven, in between finishing infant school and before joining junior school, my parents—with me in tow—moved house; moved district. It was quite an unsettling time for the entire family. As it turned out, the move was not a success and, within nine months, my parents had returned to our original neighbourhood, and I returned to all my old friends and the junior school I would have joined if we had never moved away. But a lot can happen in nine months. During that time, almost all my old friends had joined the Cubs, and I had not. On the whole, I was none too bothered about this state of affairs: I had no great desire to do Cub-type activities; I didn't want to collect badges for washing cars or identifying flowers; and I had a nascent suspicion that all Cub Akelas were paedophiles—a fiction born out to be fact in the case of our local troop. However, the one arena where I did feel a sense of great injustice and personal victimisation due to my non-Cub status was at the end of our school's weekly country dancing lesson—I ask you, what kind of school possesses its own maypole outside of Summerisle? At the end of the country dance lesson, the teacher—a short, elderly woman in spectacles—got everyone to sit cross-legged on the floor. She would then permit the Girl Guides to leave first; after them, the Boy Scouts could leave; then the Girl Brownies; then the Boy Cubs; until left, still sitting on their hands, would be a rag-tag assembly of non-conformists, who lived outside of accepted society. After receiving fierce glares all around from behind her spectacles, finally we stragglers would be granted our freedom. And why was this so galling? Because country dance class fell immediately before lunchtime and, by the time we were released, all the best food in the school canteen had already been snaffled.

The Joy of Reading First Editions

What is special about first editions? What makes these books the particular prize of all book collectors? There is an obvious rarity value associated with them, which makes them desirable; in some cases, it is a question of going back to the original text, which might have been altered or abridged in a later edition; I think there is something else, too. It is an undefinable connection—to the author; to the past; to a passing moment in time; an individuality, which imbues a first edition with a unique quality missing in later, mass-produced imprints.

For me, there are few things more wonderful than holding a first edition of one of the 'big brick' Biggles books published by Oxford University Press. It is almost fetishistic. The thought that the book has survived nearly ninety years; the different hands that it will have passed through; the history it will have experienced; the bookshelves it will have sat on; the different people who will have read it. Historian David Olusoga recently presented a BBC series called *A House Through Time*, which looked at an ordinary house in four different British cities—Liverpool; Newcastle; Bristol; and Leeds—in the context of the life stories of its tenants through history, but I think that a similarly rich vein of social history could be discovered by tracing the various ownerships of an old Biggles first edition. By reading these first editions, you add your own impressions and experiences to the baton, and form a new chain in the relay race between past and future.

These big old Biggles books are also blessed with drawings to illustrate the text, which are sometimes missing from later editions. The Oxford books typically include a colour frontispiece, and half a dozen or so black and white illustrations throughout the book. I have often been amused by the choice of the scene that is depicted in these images; although, sometimes, it will be a depiction of a dramatic moment from the book—such as the attack by the giant squid in *Biggles in the South Seas* (p. 105)—often, it is a rather dull scene—like Biggles first meeting with the Maltovian Ambassador in *Biggles Goes to War* (p. 12). Nevertheless, an illustration is always welcome, and adds to the individual nature of the book; to that undefinable quality that makes a first edition 'special'.

Facsimile Dust Wrappers

Love them or loathe them, facsimile dust wrappers manage to divide opinion.

To track down a first edition copy of an old Biggles book is often difficult enough; to track down one complete with its original dust jacket is sometimes nigh on impossible. Libraries often remove dust jackets for reasons known only to themselves; and Age and innumerable little boys' grubby fingers account for so many of the delicate wrappers, which get torn, creased, scuffed and ruckled all in the course of their duty to help protect the book, which lies beneath.

Debate rages amongst book collectors—and, let me tell you, some of those book collectors know how to rage—concerning the merits—or otherwise—of adding facsimile dust wrappers to books, which are missing their original covers. Personally, I am all for facsimile dust wrappers. If I can't find a copy with an original wrapper, it still gives me great joy to add a facsimile cover to a volume, so that I can experience something of the excitement of how it would have felt to have read the book in its original state. The illustrations on some of these wrappers—particularly the early ones from Oxford University Press by Howard Leigh—are iconic pieces of art in their own right.

Of course, I recognise the arguments against facsimile wrappers. Collectors are concerned that facsimiles will be passed off for originals; that exorbitant prices will be charged for books that don't warrant them. In my experience, this has never been the case. Books with facsimile wrappers are clearly described as such, and priced accordingly; in most cases, professionally-produced facsimiles will have the fact printed clearly on them, so that there can be no possible way to mistake them for originals.

Now, I am never going to suggest that a facsimile wrapper would be better than finding a book with its original wrapper intact but, if you can't find diamonds, I am perfectly happy with a spot of zirconia.

Asterisks and Pyramids

The identification of first editions is often a tricky business. Where some publishers make it easy by following an established convention; others appear to go out of their way to confuse the issue. Of the four main imprints under which the Biggles series was first published—John Hamilton, Oxford University Press, Hodder and Stoughton, and Brockhampton Press—there is the typical variation in approach.

The early Hamilton books are perhaps the hardest to correctly identify taking into account only the evidence of the book itself. They tend to be undated, and often it is only possible to recognise the individual edition by other factors, such as the catalogue of books listed in the rear of the volume, or the position of the text on the spine of the binding. Now that there is a wealth of information available on the internet to aid identification of the Hamilton volumes, the process is greatly simplified.

Peculiarly, it is the Oxford volumes that tend to be the ones most routinely muddled, and this despite the fact that Oxford have a clear and consistent way of marking their editions. First editions are clearly dated on the verso of the title page, following the word 'Printed'. Later editions are similarly dated, following the word 'Reprinted'. The Oxford editions also operate a system of asterisks. First editions have no asterisks; first reprints have one asterisks printed at the bottom right hand corner of the title page; second reprints, two asterisks. There are anomalies, but this is a good general rule. The confusion seems to stem from the 'Pyramid' and 'Flying Jacket' editions. These are all later reprints, but often display on the verso of their title page a statement that reads as though they are a first printing. The 'pyramid' nomenclature comes from the fact that the front boards of these volumes illustrate a plane flying over a background of pyramids and palm trees; the 'flying jacket' from the image on the dust wrapper of Biggles in full flying garb.

The Hodder volumes tend to be clearly marked, detailing reprint information on the verso of the title page; similarly, the Brockhampton first editions are readily identifiable, although books with laminated pictorial boards or ones that state they are part of the 'Hampton Library' are reprints.

Reading #21: *Biggles in the Gobi*

Screw you, Mr Arundel Bookseller, who made me cry when I was just a young boy (see *A Disappointment in Arundel*). Screw you! Has my entire life been leading up to this moment of retribution? That copy of *Biggles in the Gobi* that was denied me then, is now mine for the reading. And has it all been worth it? It is a lot of pressure to put on one book and, like *Biggles and the Leopards of Zinn*, the reality is maybe not quite as exciting as the promise.

In the foreword to *Biggles in the Gobi*, W. E. Johns makes a bold claim: "All the places named in the following pages really exist." (p. 8). I was intrigued to discover if this was true. I know very little about places in the Gobi, so if Johns was playing fast and loose with the truth, I would be in no position to denounce him, so a bit of research was going to be required. First, Johns mentions the scene of the novel is close to the town of Tunhwang. This is the modern-day city of Dunhuang, in Gansu Province, in western China, and commands a key strategic position on the ancient Silk Road, with routes towards India, Mongolia, Tibet and Siberia. The Tang River, which Johns claims it sits upon, is the Danghe River, and its two most famous landmarks are Crescent Moon Spring, an oasis five kilometres south of Dunhuang—referred to by Johns as the Lake of the Crescent Moon— and the Mogao Caves, which lie twenty-five kilometres southeast of the same city, and which are also known as the Thousand Buddha Grottoes or—as Johns refers to them—the Caves of the Thousand Buddhas. There is no faulting Johns' geography. Today, the Mogao Caves are a UNESCO World Heritage Site, and form a complex of over 500 temples with examples of Buddhist art from the 4th to the 14th centuries. It is good to know that the site is preserved today, considering how close they came to being blown up in *Biggles in the Gobi*!

The region of China that Johns describes has a long history of conflict, and two particular passages from the book struck me as resonating with contemporary events. The first takes me away from the region, with an assertion made by Ginger: "'The British Government has never jibbed at paying for service, and as all the world knows it has never failed to pay its debts.'" (p. 73). That statement may have been true at the time that Johns wrote it, but a subsequent world event changed matters: in the 1970s, the Shah of Iran, Mohammad Reza Pahlavi, placed an order with the British government for 1,500 Chieftain tanks and 250 Armoured Recovery Vehicles, at a cost of some £650M. In 1979, at the time that the Shah was disposed by Ayatollah Khomeini, only a small amount of the order had been fulfilled, and the debt for the undelivered part of the order never repaid. Until very recently. The British government paid £393.8M to the Iranians in March 2022 in repayment of their long-outstanding debt 'in parallel' with the release of British citizen Nazanin Zaghari-Ratcliffe, who had been held captive by the Iranians since 2016. Returning to China, and 2022, the United Nations filed a report talking of grave human rights violations by the Chinese against the Uyghur minority group in the Xinjiang Uyghur Autonomous Region in northwest China, not far from the setting for *Biggles in the Gobi*; Johns makes reference to the region: "…near the junction of Sinkiang and Mongolia." (p. 16). At the time that Johns was writing the book, it was another minority group, the Kyrgyz—or Kirghiz, as Johns writes—who were facing persecution: "'They say they've heard that many more soldiers have arrived in Tunhwang, and the Tiger has given orders that all Kirghiz are to be hunted down and exterminated.'" (p. 127). It is over sixty years since *Biggles in the Gobi* was first published and, in some matters, not a lot has changed during that time. But, then, Time is a very strange entity, all of its own. What is the ontology of Time?

Ginger becomes quite philosophical on the subject: "He lost all count of time. In some strange way such manmade sections of it as hours and minutes seemed no longer to have meaning." (p. 78). Ginger is undoubtedly correct when he talks about hours and minutes having no meaning, or, at least, they only have the meaning that humans have attributed to them; they are a social construct. But is all time a social construct? Humans perceive time as a process of change. As the British physicist Julian Barbour states, we have no evidence of the past other than our memory of it, and no evidence of the future other than our belief in it. It has long been commonplace to talk about Time being the fourth dimension. But, what does that really mean for creatures who inhabit a three-dimensional world? Massachusetts Institute of Technology physicist Max Tegmark describes the 'block universe' theory where rather than describing reality as a three-dimensional place where stuff happens over time, it is a four-dimensional place where nothing happens, because it is all already all there at the same time—past, present and future. This is also known as eternalism. For some reason, this idea has a resonance of truth for me. Admittedly, it makes the last twenty minutes I have just spent typing this paragraph, or the five minutes that you have spent reading it, a bit of a 'waste of time' when it already exists somewhere but, hey-ho, wasting time is nothing new; I have long admired the quote from Shakespeare's *Richard II*: "I wasted time, and now doth time waste me." (*Richard II*, Act V Scene V).

Past, present and future: all equally 'real'; all equally 'now'. My dad listening out for doodlebugs (see *My Dad's War*); W. E. Johns finishing the last sentence of *Biggles in the Gobi*: "As the Air-Commodore remarked when they were back at the Yard, they couldn't do more, or less." (p. 160); me crying in the bookshop in Arundel.

So, all the more chance that the Arundel bookseller might hear me when I say: "Screw you!"

Marks of Ownership

Maybe it was all the speculation about the nature of Time, that got me thinking about some of the old first edition books in my own Biggles collection and who had previously owned them.

Some collectors attempt to obtain pristine copies of the books in their collection, but I rather like the signs of other readers' past ownership: a name scrawled on the first page in an obviously juvenile hand; the inscription of a gift from loving relatives; a bookplate declaring that the copy had been awarded as a prize. For me, all these marks add to the history of the particular volume; trace a path from publication through to my own hands.

It is with a sense of poignancy, that I am conscious that many of those 'juvenile hands' who scrawled their names in some of the old Oxford University Press books in my collection will now be long dead. My copy of *Biggles Hits the Trail* has the name H. C. Richford inside, followed by the date 1936. The name is written in ink, in neat capital letters, neatly centred at the top of the first page of the book. I wonder about H. C. Richford. Boy or girl? There is no clue in the simple inscription. What was he/she like? What did he/she go on to do? In an age before the internet, my speculation would have ended there, never to be rewarded with the answers to my questions. However, a quick Google search brings up some compelling evidence, which helps to populate the biography of the previous owner of my book. An online obituary states that Squadron Leader Hugh Christopher Richford died in 2007 aged 84. He was a pilot with 514 Squadron RAF flying Avro Lancaster bombers during the Second World War when he was awarded the DFC, and later flew with 207 Squadron, where he took part in the Suez campaign flying Vickers Valiant B.1s. At the time that he wrote his name in my copy of *Biggles Hits the Trail* he would have been thirteen years old. He would not have known precisely what career lay ahead of him although, like my old friend Gary (see *My Best Friend the Pilot*) perhaps he already had a good idea of what he wanted to become; certainly, his reading of W. E. Johns suggests an early interest in aviation; his life, hopefully, one of ambition fulfilled.

Reading #22: *Biggles Looks Back*

This is something of a rarity: a Biggles love story. The book provides the conclusion to an episode in Biggles' early life related in the short story *Affaire de Coeur*, first published in *The Camels are Coming* and later reprinted in *Biggles, Pioneer Air Fighter* (The Thames Publishing Co., 1954). It also deals with a relationship, which provides much of the inspiration for John Pearson's fictionalised biography of Biggles. For me, the final words of *Affaire de Coeur* are some of the most poignant that W. E. Johns ever wrote: "Got my fingers burnt a bit too." It is typical Biggles understatement; the dual meaning summing up in six brief words his near death in a bombing raid and the experience of being betrayed by the woman he loved.

The incidents related in *Affaire de Coeur* occur during Biggles' time stationed in France during the First World War as a member of 266 Squadron. However, by the time that Johns wrote *Biggles Looks Back* (Hodder, 1965) a period of 47 years had elapsed since the end of the First World War, a time during which a second world war had taken place. It is perhaps as a consequence of this that Johns rather blurs which earlier war he is referring to; he talks about the annexation of the Sudetenland, and the creation of the Protectorate of Bohemia and Moravia, incidents from the Second rather than the First World War: "They served only on the Western Front, not in the East, so they never found themselves in conflict with old friends in Czechoslovakia." (p. 66). And the illustration of Biggles recalling the bombing raid that occurred in *Affair de Coeur* (p. 18). shows a jet plane looking suspiciously like a Gloucester Meteor of 1940s vintage, rather than something like a Gotha G.V or a Zeppelin-Staaken R. VI, which might have been more likely to have carried out the raid as described. Of course, this would all have had something to do with the problem of Biggles' age, which has sometimes been a criticism levelled at the books. Biggles was born in 1899; at the end of the First World War he was nineteen; however, by the time that Johns wrote *Biggles Looks Back*, he would have been 66. Plenty young enough to still enjoy a dalliance with an old flame, but maybe not quite young enough to realistically engage in the river-wading, castle-storming, ivy-climbing antics that he was required to undertake in order to encounter her.

Accompanying Biggles on his search for his missing love is Bertie. In stating his credentials for the mission—"'My civilian passport should command a little respectful attention. I mean my title's on it. Had to be. The Lord Lissie, Chedcombe Manor. Occupation, gentleman, and all that rot, if you see what I mean.'"––I am reminded of the nameless protagonist in Geoffrey Household's classic thriller novel *Rogue Male* (Chatto, 1939). Household's hero is an aristocratic sportsman who endeavours to hunt down a similarly nameless European dictator—presumably Hitler. He must venture across Europe assuming the 'guise of an innocent traveller, in the same way that Biggles and Bertie voyage beyond the Iron Curtain into Czechoslovakia disguised as commercial salesmen in high quality glass ware.

However, it is another kind of literature that Johns returns to frequently throughout the book, and that is the genre of fairy tales. No doubt inspired by the dark ancient forests of the Bohemian landscape, Johns makes reference to the works of the Brothers Grimm and populates his story with "…dreadful castles, spooky forests, and maidens in distress." (p. 76). Given the circumstances, it is perhaps appropriate that the book ends with the words: "…live happily ever after." (p. 191).

A Personal Book Hunt

As Biggles looked back, so I found myself looking back. Where I had once speculated about the inscription made by H. C. Richford in my copy of *Biggles Hits the Trail* (see *Marks of Ownership),* now I found myself speculating if there might not be similar marks left by my own dad in one of the Biggles books that he had owned as a child? Or, if not his own name written in the front of a book, perhaps an inscription to him from a relative gifting the book as a present? It seemed quite possible. But where to start looking?

I returned to my own collection of books; industry, like charity, begins at home. I could not recall a book with my dad's name in it in my own collection but, then again, I had never really looked. The number of volumes to check was not great; I was only really interested in those big old tomes published by Oxford University Press from the late-Thirties to the early-Forties. The window of possibility was narrow. Five minutes, and a dozen or so books later, and I knew that I had drawn a blank. Not that I expected anything else. To believe that I could have succeeded in my quest so easily would have been presumptuous and, for the collector in me, also rather disappointing.

By now, though, my passion for the chase was ignited. I could feel the old thrill of the hunt coursing through my veins. The desire to own an old Biggles book that had once been owned by my own dad was great. A book that he had actually read as a child; a book he would have enjoyed; perhaps one that had temporarily stayed the fear of actual warfare, as he read it avidly beneath the bedclothes on a cold, wartime night. This was more than just trying to hunt out a first edition copy of an early Biggles book; it was attempting to locate one particular book amongst those first editions, and with only the haziest clues by which to identify it. An impossible task? Possibly. But I continued undaunted.

Logic demanded that what I needed was a lot of Biggles first editions. The greater the number of books, the more likely that I would discover one that had belonged to my dad. And who do I know who has the largest number of Biggles books? Roger Harris, who runs the excellent biggles.com website. Very kindly, Roger looked through all the relevant volumes in his collection, which covered the appropriate period; all 143 of them, but without success. However, he had a very useful suggestion to make:

"Just check Biggles books on eBay and see who they are dedicated to...."

Very soon, I was scouring through the listings on eBay of all the Biggles books published by Oxford University Press. It was a long list, which I wondered whether could be shortened. The problem was that many of the listings simply didn't show pictures of the early pages of the book where any inscriptions might lie; plenty of front cover photographs, but not so many prelims. However, there was a direct correlation between the value of the book and the number of photographs posted about it; the more expensive the book the more photographs. Accordingly, I filtered my eBay search to list the books in order of most expensive first, and began searching again. Still no luck. I moved on to abebooks.com and repeated the same procedure.

And, after looking through only about half a dozen books, I found what I was looking for, although I didn't recognise it as such at first. I had been scanning so many images of books, and dust wrappers, and front pages that my mind was becoming a bit jaded; I was acting like an automaton; seeing, but not really seeing the image that was in front of me; mechanically, moving onto the next. It was in this mode that I flicked past an image of a small inscription on the front page of a particular book, barely reading the words written, before moving onto another picture. It was only a minute or two later that my subconscious mind alerted me to something that it had noticed. I went back, began to read the inscription again.

The book was the 'thin' third edition of *Biggles Sees It Through*, complete with original dust wrapper. The wrapper was a little bit worn at the edges, but it was not in bad condition for its age. The listing showed four pictures, the third one being a small inscription at the top of the first page: "ALAN. From Grandad. Xmas 1943." It was not conclusive, but it was enough. The name was right; the date was right; the occasion was right. One other tiny piece of 'evidence' was that the location of the bookseller who was advertising the book was right for where my dad would have been living at the time.

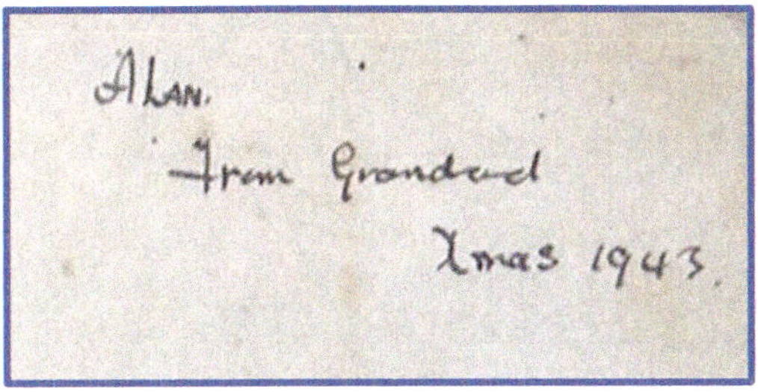

I knew that there could be other Alans, other Grandads, other people who had received Biggles books for Christmas presents in 1943 but, ultimately, all that mattered was that I *believed* that this was one of my dad's own books.

And did I buy the book from the bookseller advertising it on abebooks? You must be joking! It was £480! I'm not going to shell out that kind of money unless it's a dead cert.

Spanning the Generations

Where my dad led and I followed, what of my own son? Solemnly, I hung on to many of my old childhood paperbacks—not just Biggles, but 'William' books, too––in the mistaken belief that when my son reached the age when he could read, that he would be as thrilled and entertained by them as was I. How wrong could I be. The incidents related in the books were no longer current to a Millennial generation; there were greater distractions in Playstation and Youtube and playing football. As far as Biggles is concerned, I am the end of the line.

However, Biggles does live on. It is interesting to see recent hardcover reprints of *Biggles Sees It Though* and *Biggles in the Baltic* by publishers Canelo, plus a whole plethora of Kindle editions. I am intrigued to see where is the market for these new volumes. As a traditionalist, I am not a great fan of Kindle, preferring the experience of reading a physical book to an electronic one and, nowadays, I am much more likely to hunt out an old edition rather than buy a new one, but it is good to see that a publisher has been prepared to breathe new life into Biggles, even though neither me nor my son might be at the front of the queue to buy one.

Reading #23: *Biggles – Secret Agent*

My final reading choice—*Biggles – Secret Agent* (Oxford, 1940)—is a step back into Biggles' past. And a step back for no better reason than it is one of my favourite stories from the Biggles series.

It has all the ingredients of a classic adventure story: a threat to world security; a deadly secret mission; a dangerous, undercover journey behind enemy lines; a spooky old castle, full of secret passages and underground tunnels; and a clearly defined enemy, in the shape of the *Sturmabteilung*, the original paramilitary wing of the German Nazi Party. In terms of its story of infiltration into enemy territory and its central European castle location, there are similarities between this story and *Biggles Looks Back*. Another shared theme is the reference to *Grimm's Fairy Tales*, a copy of the book even turning up in the unlikely location of a coffin in an old graveyard vault.

The story is rare, for the times, to describe a Jewish character facing persecution at the hands of an oppressive, invading regime. When Biggles and Ginger enter the village of Unterhamstadt, Ginger sees the word 'Jude' scrawled on a door: "'What does that mean?' he asked—'The owner of the place is a Jew. Apparently this is one of the places under the influence of anti-Jewish propaganda.'" (p. 53). While most of the world was still turning a blind eye to the anti-Semitic legislation and attacks on Jewish properties and persons orchestrated by Hitler's government, it was more typical for children's stories to unthinkingly reflect the attitudes of the time, perhaps most graphically seen in the Richmal Crompton short story 'William and the Nasties', which appeared in *William the Detective* (Newnes, 1935), where William and his gang of Outlaws are shown to persecute a Jewish sweet shop owner. W. E. Johns' more authentic depiction must have been quite shocking at the time: '"Observe what persecution and the fear of death does to a man."' (p. 58).

Once again, Biggles finds himself pitted against his old adversary Erich von Stalhein, and the roots of their later 'bromance', which is apparent in *Biggles Looks Back*, are evident even here. Both men display a grudging respect for each other, and both admire certain qualities that the other possesses, but there is one area where Biggles finds von Stalhein lacking: '"There is one quality he lacks and that's imagination."' (p. 145).

If there is one quality that I like to believe that I possess, it is imagination. I do not have the practical abilities of my dad, or the artistic abilities of my son. I do not have the work ethic that they both possess, or the courage, or the resilience, or the social responsibility. They would both make better Biggles than I. But, in the absence of other redeeming qualities, I can always fall back on the fact that I am possessed with imagination. I have long considered imagination to be a blessing; I can scarcely think of a greater one. It has taken me to wonderful places; introduced me to amazing people; kept me enthralled with extraordinary stories. For people who do not inhabit the 'world of the mind', it might seem like an unfathomable indulgence, or even an impenetrable fortress, but I consider myself fortunate to have lived a 'second life' more in fiction than in fact. I have always been fascinated by zoologist and anthropologist Lyall Watson's account of his paleontological discovery on a beach in southern Africa of a small, ancient human skeleton with a proportionally large skull, which he christened a Strandloper. He pictured the Strandloper as an evolutionary offshoot of *homo sapiens* possessed of limited physical attributes, but blessed with an extraordinary gift of imagination, capable of living a full and rich life within the mind. The Strandloper might be considered an evolutionary dead-end or, just perhaps, it might be a glimpse of our own future, as we embrace a world increasingly more virtual than real?

Farewell Mildred

For the number of mentions she has received in the second half of this book, anyone could be forgiven for thinking that Mildred vacated the premises some little time ago but, contrary to appearances, she has remained an omnipresent companion throughout; the devil at my shoulder; the nagging critic who forces me to reassess the Biggles books on a different level other than one of pure enjoyment.

However, the longer that I have spent in Mildred's company, I find myself becoming the critic and not, as Mildred might like, a critic of Biggles or of W. E. Johns, but of Mildred herself.

Book burning has a long history, and none of it is very glorious. The term 'cancel culture' might only have gained traction within the last decade, but the concept has been around for millennia. More recent times have seen book burning in Nazi Germany; by followers of Mao during the Cultural Revolution; of copies of Salman Rushdie's *The Satanic Verses*; and even copies of Harry Potter in the US. If it can be believed that you can judge a person by the company that they keep, Mildred might like to reconsider her bedfellows.

Cancel culture divides opinion into two distinct camps, each desperately battling for the moral high ground. On the one side are those who believe that it gives a platform for marginalised and disenfranchised voices, on the other protectors of free speech and open debate. Whilst there are clearly certain 'voices' who deliberately propagate hate and division and which it might seem preferable not to hear, on the whole I am of the opinion that it is a more dangerous society if we prevent freedom of speech, as can be witnessed in any number of repressive regimes around the world who operate this policy. Ultimately, it is the 'cancel culture' mentality that leads to intolerance, authoritarianism, and a denial of history, which prevents us from learning from the mistakes of the past.

Within the realms of Literature—an expansive term, in which I very much include the works of W. E. Johns—suppression of freedom of expression can only sound the death knell for original thought. The best-selling Nigerian author, Chimamanda

Ngozi Adichie talked both very eloquently and very passionately on this subject during her Reith Lecture 2022 entitled 'Freedom of Speech'. While discussing social censure and cancel culture in terms of them being a more covert and dishonest form of authoritarianism, Adichie said: "This new social censure demands consensus, while being wilfully blind to its own tyranny. I think it portends the death of curiosity, the death of learning, and the death of creativity."

I enjoyed J. K. Rowling's Twitter responses to people who had burned her books: "…I've still got your money, so by all means borrow my lighter."; and "…you can lead a girl to books about the rise and fall of an autocrat, but you still can't make her think." In the current climate of mob rule on social media, it is only someone with Rowling's clout who can stand up and continue to say what she *really* thinks.

And it is with this same thought, that I will bid *adieu* to Mildred. My prevailing emotion is one of sorrow for her. Because of her belief in the practice of book-burning, she will never have discovered how to filter dirty water through a piece of burnt toast; she will never know how to distinguish the different sounds made by a Rolls-Royce Merlin engine and a Daimler-Benz one; and she will never have experienced the simple, youthful pleasure of reading one of Johns' wonderful adventure yarns, from cover to cover, at one sitting.

Biggles is Good

I began this book with the suggestion that Biggles might be bad. Many people, I acknowledge, will adhere to that view—although many of those same people will never have read a single Biggles book. I couched the premise of this book as though it was entered in the spirit of an open investigation; having reached the conclusion of this book, I can now admit that that stance was an utter sham. I was hugely biased from the start. How could I be otherwise? My seven-year old self was already an advocate. I was never likely to change my opinion even given a generation of alternative views. I might be discovered to be wrong in my beliefs––Time tends to reveal that everything anyone ever believed was wrong; but, at least, I will never be found to be a hypocrite. I always believed that Biggles was good.

It is a rare blessing to maintain a friendship, which lasts a lifetime, and I have Biggles and W. E. Johns to thank for their constancy in that respect. I was a child with Biggles; I am now an adult with Biggles; I have grown up with Biggles—although my wife might maintain that I have actually always remained a child with Biggles.

Both Biggles and Johns have added enormously to my education. I learned things from them that I would never have acquired in the course of my formal schooling. General knowledge that I would never have come across by any other means; an excitement about the world and its endless diversity and possibilities; an interest in other lands and cultures outside of my everyday experience. My experience of Life, would have been less rich without Biggles in it.

It is very fashionable to talk about the lens through which knowledge is viewed. If my lens has been through Biggles, then I accept that it comes with many of the negative prejudices and outlooks, which I mentioned at the start of this book (see *Biggles is Bad?*). Plenty of other people have justified the Biggles books—and pretty much every other piece of literature from the past—as being a product of the attitudes of their times. It might seem lazy of me to passively accept this viewpoint, but the simple truth is that it is a fact. The liberal, campaigning fore-thinker of today is the stuck-in-the-mud, outdated bigot of tomorrow.

Amidst all the analysis and soul-searching, it is easy to lose sight of the fact that Johns was writing to entertain. His intention was to inspire and interest a mid-20th century audience of boys and girls. The fact that his books continue to be collected and held in such fond esteem by those same—now rather ageing—boys and girls, is proof that he achieved his ambitions manifestly. I have lost count of how many times I have read, and re-read, the Biggles books in my lifetime. They are a guilty pleasure that I routinely return to and, no matter how many times I return to a particular story, I can guarantee that I will always be entertained by it and discover new things to enjoy about it.

I recognise that I was very fortunate to enjoy a stable and loving childhood, and I like the way that the Biggles books provide a bridge between my adult life and many of those fond childhood memories. Books are more than just the sum of their words and stories; they are an experience, which requires a certain amount of effort and a degree of time expended and, as such, they contain the memories of *where* and *when* they were read, and *what* other things were happening at the time of reading.

I know that whatever I am doing during the rest of my life that I shall periodically return to my Biggles books and, like the loyal and dependable friend that he is, I know that whenever I come calling he will be there waiting for me.

A Biggles Bibliography

Not really a bibliography; just a list. Not even an exhaustive list. Just a list. The kind of list that would have appealed to me as a child; the kind of list, which regularly appeared on the back cover, or the front pages of many a Biggles book, and which always whetted my appetite to want to read the other books in the series, which I had never come across before.

The Camels are Coming (John Hamilton Ltd, 1932)
The Cruise of the Condor (Hamilton, 1933)
Biggles of the Camel Squadron (Hamilton, 1934)
Biggles Flies Again (Hamilton, 1934)
The Black Peril (Hamilton, 1935)
Biggles Learns to Fly (Amalgamated Press, 1935)
Biggles Hits the Trail (Oxford University Press, 1935)
Biggles Flies East (Oxford, 1935)
Biggles in France (Amalgamated Press, 1935)
Biggles & Co (Oxford, 1936)
Biggles in Africa (Oxford, 1936)
Biggles – Air Commodore (Oxford, 1937)
Biggles Flies West (Oxford, 1937)
Biggles Goes to War (Oxford, 1938)
Biggles Flies South (Oxford, 1938)
Biggles Flies North (Oxford, 1939)
The Rescue Flight (Oxford, 1939)
Biggles in Spain (Oxford, 1939)
Biggles – Secret Agent (Oxford, 1940)
Biggles in the South Seas (Oxford, 1940)
Biggles in the Baltic (Oxford, 1940)
Biggles Defies the Swastika (Oxford, 1941)
Biggles Sees It Through (Oxford, 1941)
Spitfire Parade (Oxford, 1941)
Biggles in the Jungle (Oxford, 1942)
Biggles Sweeps the Desert (Hodder and Stoughton, 1942)
Biggles – Charter Pilot (Oxford, 1943)
Biggles in Borneo (Oxford, 1943)
Biggles Fails to Return (Hodder, 1943)
Biggles in the Orient (Hodder, 1945)

A Biggles Bibliography

Biggles Delivers the Goods (Hodder, 1946)
Sergeant Bigglesworth CID (Hodder, 1947)
Biggles' Second Case (Hodder, 1948)
Biggles Hunts Big Game (Hodder, 1948)
Biggles Takes a Holiday (Hodder, 1949)
Biggles Breaks the Silence (Hodder, 1949)
Biggles Gets His Men (Hodder, 1950)
Another Job for Biggles (Hodder, 1951)
Biggles Goes to School (Hodder, 1951)
Biggles Works It Out (Hodder, 1951)
Biggles Takes the Case (Hodder, 1952)
Biggles Follows On (Hodder, 1952)
Biggles and the Black Raider (Hodder, 1953)
Biggles in the Blue (Brockhampton Press, 1953)
Biggles in the Gobi (Hodder, 1953)
Biggles Cuts It Fine (Hodder, 1954)
Biggles and the Pirate Treasure (Brockhampton, 1954)
Biggles Foreign Legionnaire (Hodder, 1954)
Biggles in Australia (Hodder, 1955)
Biggles' Chinese Puzzle (Brockhampton, 1955)
No Rest for Biggles (Hodder, 1956)
Biggles Takes Charge (Brockhampton, 1956)
Biggles Makes Ends Meet (Hodder, 1957)
Biggles of the Interpol (Brockhampton, 1957)
Biggles on the Home Front (Hodder, 1957)
Biggles Presses On (Brockhampton, 1958)
Biggles on Mystery Island (Hodder, 1958)
Biggles Buries a Hatchet (Brockhampton, 1958)
Biggles in Mexico (Brockhampton, 1959)
Biggles' Combined Operation (Hodder, 1959)
Biggles at World's End (Brockhampton, 1959)
Biggles and the Leopards of Zinn (Brockhampton, 1960)
Biggles Goes Home (Hodder, 1960)
Biggles and the Poor Rich Boy (Brockhampton, 1961)
Biggles Forms a Syndicate (Hodder, 1961)
Biggles and the Missing Millionaire (Brockhampton, 1961)
Biggles Goes Alone (Hodder, 1962)

Orchids for Biggles (Brockhampton, 1962)
Biggles Sets a Trap (Hodder, 1962)
Biggles Takes It Rough (Brockhampton, 1963)
Biggles Takes a Hand (Hodder, 1963)
Biggles' Special Case (Brockhampton, 1963)
Biggles and the Plane That Disappeared (Hodder, 1963)
Biggles and the Lost Sovereigns (Brockhampton, 1964)
Biggles and the Black Mask (Hodder, 1964)
Biggles Investigates (Brockhampton, 1964)
Biggles Looks Back (Hodder, 1965)
Biggles and the Plot That Failed (Brockhampton, 1965)
Biggles and the Blue Moon (Brockhampton, 1965)
Biggles Scores a Bull (Hodder, 1965)
Biggles in the Terai (Brockhampton, 1966)
Biggles and the Gun Runners (Brockhampton, 1966)
Biggles Sorts It Out (Brockhampton, 1967)
Biggles and the Penitent Thief (Brockhampton, 1967)
Biggles and the Deep Blue Sea (Brockhampton, 1968)
Biggles in the Underworld (Brockhampton, 1968)
Biggles and the Little Green God (Brockhampton, 1969)
Biggles and the Noble Lord (Brockhampton, 1969)
Biggles and the Dark Intruder (Brockhampton, 1970)
Biggles Sees Too Much (Brockhampton, 1970)
Biggles Does Some Homework (Norman Wright, 1998)

Printed in Great Britain
by Amazon

19069248R00108